# BLOCKCHAIN

## The Crypto Revolution

Discover the Fantastic World of Cryptocurrencies and Blockchain With the Best Guide for Beginners to Investing and Understanding the new Global age of Finance

**NATHAN HARRISON**

bng-books.com

# Acknowledgment

*I want to thank you for buying my book and for trusting me, sincerely... Thanks!*

I hope you enjoy my work and help you to always look forward!

## *Happy Trading !!*

Again… Thank you!

## Nathan Harrison

## Click to see all my books

**bng-books.com**

# TABLE OF CONTENTS

# Introduction

Twelve years after its birth, blockchain today represents a paradigm and an innovation platform that allows us to give new answers to the many and diverse needs of businesses, organizations, citizens and consumers. If for several years the knowledge and attention towards the blockchain has been mainly limited to the world of developers or in other respects to those who had immediately glimpsed its potential from a financial point of view, in the last year there has been an important leap in quality in terms of dissemination of knowledge and expectations. The blockchain, as it happened for the Internet, is gradually entering our lives, often indirectly, in many cases only as a possible solution to platforms that solve in an innovative way our needs or the needs of the companies in which we work, or of Public Administrations that provide the services we use. Whatever the way in which we come into contact with the blockchain, it seems increasingly important to know it, to be aware of its prospects and its potential.

In particular, unlike other technological innovations, the blockchain refers to some apparently very different and distant themes and concepts, which we do not normally associate with digital innovation: trust, responsibility, community, decentralization. In addition, alongside these, there are others that have a strong relationship with technology, but which in turn are not "usual" as the themes of transparency, immutability, sharing and "competition" in achieving a result. The secret of so much interest and expectations is certainly also to be found in the originality of the ingredients that make up the blockchain or that come with the blockchain.

## CHAPTER 1

# BLOCKCHAIN

It is difficult to classify the blockchain in a single definition. The blockchain can be read and presented from different points of view and from different perspectives. In this book we will see different ones. The following is a first definition that relates to the technology family in which this technology is placed.

The blockchain is a subfamily of technologies in which the register is structured as a chain of blocks containing transactions and whose validation is entrusted to a consensus mechanism, distributed on all nodes of the network in the case of permissionless or public blockchains, or on all nodes that are authorized to participate in the transaction validation process to be included in the register in the case of permissioned or private blockchains.

The main characteristics of blockchain technologies are the immutability of the register, transparency, traceability of transactions and security based on cryptographic techniques.

The blockchain is based on a network and from the point of view of functionality it allows to manage a database in a distributed way. From an operational point of view, it is an alternative to centralized archives and allows you to manage the updating of data with the collaboration of network participants and with the possibility of having shared, accessible, distributed data among all participants. In fact, it should be repeated, it allows data management in terms of verification and authorization without the need for a central authority.

In trying to understand what the blockchain is, in many cases we will rely on the definitions that are proposed, trying to qualify them. For some, blockchain is the next generation of the internet, or better yet, the New Internet. It is believed that it may represent a kind of Internet of Transactions. These definitions tend to combine the blockchain with the Internet of individuals, or the Internet of the people we use and frequent every day, which in turn has extended to the Internet of Things to create and represent the Internet of Value on the basis of seven features: decentralization, transparency, safety, immutability, consent, responsibility and programmability.

Starting from these principles, the blockchain has become the digital declination of a new concept of trust to the point that some believe that the blockchain can also take on a value for certain aspects of a "social and political" type. In this case, the blockchain is to be seen as a platform that allows the development and realization of a new form of social relationship, which thanks to the participation of all is able to guarantee everyone the possibility of verifying, of "controlling", of having total transparency on the acts and decisions, which are recorded in archives that have the characteristic of being unalterable, unchangeable and therefore immune from corruption.

For a certain period, the blockchain was identified with the Bitcoin blockchain, that is, with the first blockchain (which is identified with a capital "B"). This identification was also superimposed on that with the Bitcoin cryptocurrency and led to a bit of "confusing" the blockchain with other areas of innovation such as digital currency. Perhaps for the latter reason, the blockchain has often been associated with an alternative or complementary digital currency concept and digital payment. In reality, as we will see, the blockchain is a much broader and more complex phenomenon.

**What is the blockchain for?**

The blockchain is (also) a solution to create unique digital assets. To understand the opportunities of the blockchain it is important to consider the issue of the uniqueness of digital assets. This is a theme that we will also see later when we address "double spending", but which can already help us understand the meaning and importance of the blockchain. But let's start with a common example. If we write a text on a word document, that text is on our computer and it is unique. When we send it to a colleague, that same text as well as on our computer will be present on a mail server and on our colleague's computer. We already have a series of duplications of the same document. That text can then of course be shared in turn and sent to other subjects who will in turn have a copy. As we all know there are no limits to this duplication and as we all know that same document can be modified and changed. Our word document is a digital asset and as it appears evident it is certainly not unique: it "started" from our computer and perhaps in a very short time it has multiplied into thousands of copies.

That same asset encrypted in a blockchain ledger could become a single asset. Exactly like in the physical world: if we pass the same document written in word printed on paper to a colleague, we lose possession of it, that document leaves our control to enter the domain of a colleague. In other words: if in the digital world the transition automatically implies a duplication, the blockchain allows you to "regain" the concept of scarcity of real world assets in the digital world and when a digital asset is passed through the blockchain (ours document) from our computer to a colleague, that document is no longer in our possession and is entirely in the hands of our colleague.

If he too needs to share it, he will lose possession of it in favor of another subject. The document will remain unique and it will not be possible to duplicate it. One of the characteristics of the blockchain, which will accompany us in our service, is its ability to create unique digital assets.

## The Importance of Unique Digital Assets

To understand the importance of unique digital assets, let's leave our example linked to a generic word document whose duplication does not involve particular problems. On the contrary, if we think of the duplication of assets that represent a value, it is clear that the guarantee of uniqueness represents an absolute value. Duplicating an asset designed to represent a currency digitally means diminishing this value to the point of canceling it. This is why the world of finance, first of all, understood the value of the blockchain in its ability to guarantee the uniqueness of a digital asset. The same value is well understood by many other sectors that are digitally representing products and services and who have in turn understood that digital allows for much more efficient management of exchanges and transactions only and exclusively if the ability to avoid duplication is guaranteed, or only if the uniqueness of the asset is guaranteed. Just like it happens in the real world.

**Blockchain and distributed ledger technology**
Before continuing, it is necessary to stop for a moment to qualify the relationship between blockchain and distributed ledger. A distinction that will accompany this service and that will help to understand some specific characteristics of the blockchain. The blockchain can be considered a technology that belongs to the category of distributed ledger technologies. Distributed ledger technology or DLT can be defined as a set of systems characterized by the fact of referring to a distributed ledger, governed in such a way as to allow access and the ability to make changes by multiple nodes of a network.

Any transaction, or the data that represents it, is subjected to an asymmetric double key signature mechanism which, although not equipped with certificates issued by accredited certifiers (the blockchain precisely provides for the overcoming of centralized certification bodies), works with a similar mechanism to that of the digital signature. DLTs provide for the use of cryptographic algorithms that enable the user to use the system by providing him with a public and a private key that is used to sign transactions or to activate smart contracts or other services connected to the blockchain. Therefore, register - distributed - or without a central validation "system or organization". The DLTs therefore envisage a validation mechanism which is in turn distributed based on the concept of consent, that is, on mechanisms that also govern this type of participation of the nodes.

The methods of managing consent together with the logics for setting the register represent two of the main qualifying points of the identity card of distributed ledger technologies, and it is within this whole that blockchains find their place.

In this case, it can be said that blockchains are distributed ledger technologies characterized by a registered set up and structured in order to manage transactions within a chain of blocks. From the point of view of the "management rules", each block is "added" to the chain on the basis of a process based on consent distributed over all the nodes of the network, or with the participation of all the nodes that are called upon to contribute to the validation of the transactions present in each block (as we will see later) and their "inclusion" in the register.

# Definitions of Blockchain

As evident, the blockchain lends itself to be interpreted. More than a technology, it is a paradigm, a way of interpreting the great theme of decentralization and participation. For this reason, as natural, there are different declinations, different interpretations and different definitions of the blockchain.
A review of definitions can be useful to understand how the blockchain is experienced and interpreted according to the perspective of use. Each definition, as we will see, highlights one or more salient aspects of the blockchain.

**Blockchain as a transaction database**
The blockchain is a technology that allows the creation and management of a large distributed database for the management of transactions that can be shared between multiple nodes of a network. It is a database structured in blocks (containing multiple transactions) which are networked together so that each transaction initiated on the network must be validated by the network itself in the "analysis" of each individual block. The blockchain is thus made up of a chain of blocks that contain multiple transactions. The solution for all transactions is entrusted to the nodes who are called to see, check and approve all transactions by creating a network that shares the archive of the entire blockchain and therefore of all the blocks with all the transactions on each node. Each block is also an archive for all transactions and for all the history of each transaction which can only be changed with the approval of the network

nodes. The transactions can be considered unchangeable (if not through the reproposal and "re-authorization" of the same by the whole network). Hence the concept of immutability.

## Blockchain as an evolution of the ledger concept

The blockchain is the realization of the distributed ledger, as an evolution from the centralized ledger, decentralized ledger up to the distributed ledger.

## Centralized ledger

The centralized logic is represented by the traditional centralized ledger with a strictly centralized One-To-Many relationship, where everything must be managed by referring to a centralized structure, authority or system.

In the centralized ledger, trust is in the authority, in the authority of the subject or system that represents the "center" of the organization.

## Decentralized ledger

The decentralized ledger re-proposes the logic of centralization at the "local" level with "satellites" organized in turn in the form of One-To-Many that relate in turn in a form that repeats the One-To-Many model. There is no longer a "big" central subject but many "central subjects". Even in this case, trust is delegated to a central subject, logically closer, but still centralized.

Organizations based on decentralized ledger define a governance that establishes forms of centralized coordination.

## Distributed ledger

The real change is represented by the distributed ledger, that is a real and complete distributed logic where there is no longer any center and where the governance logic is built around a new concept of trust between all the subjects. Nobody (but absolutely nobody) has the possibility to prevail, and the decision-making process strictly passes through a process of construction of the consensus.

## The blockchain as a database for encrypted transactions

The blockchain is a large database for the management of encrypted transactions on a decentralized peer-to-peer network that gives its name to a new technological platform, which allows us to redefine and reset the way we create, obtain and exchange value. The blockchain is doing with transactions what the Internet has done with information and it is doing it thanks to a process that combines distributed systems, advanced cryptography and game theory.

## The blockchain as a public register open to everybody

The blockchain is a decentralized database that stores assets and transactions on a peer-to-peer network. It is a public registry for managing data related to transactions present in blocks and managed by cryptography by network participants who verify, approve and subsequently record all blocks with all data of each transaction on all nodes. The same "information" is therefore present on all nodes and therefore becomes unchangeable except through an operation that requires the approval of the majority of the network nodes and which, in any case, will not change the history of that same information.

The blockchain is not an application, it is not a system, it is not a technology. The blockchain is a new paradigm for information management that allows to guarantee the real immutability of data because it is able to guarantee and certify the complete history of all data and all operations connected to each transaction.

**The blockchain as a secure and unchangeable ledger over time**

The blockchain is the decentralized and cryptographically secure ledger for managing transactions on peer-to-peer networks. That is, it is a technology that allows the exchange of information and different types of values on the internet. There are many types of transactions that can be supported and managed with the blockchain. Payment is an example, as are transactions related to the exchange of goods and services or as well as the management of information related to contracts.

## CHAPTER 2

# HISTORY OF BLOCKCHAIN

## Satoshi Nakamoto

From the moment the blockchain appeared, it immediately raised a double reaction: on the one hand, those who read this intuition in direct relation to the work of Satoshi Nakamoto, who in October 2008 published a document proposing Bitcoin as a digital currency. Nakamoto followed up on this document with the release of the first Bitcoin software in January 2009. Alongside the vision that leads to associating the blockchain with Bitcoin cryptocurrencies, there is the one that instead invites us to look up to many other applications, without placing any kind of limitation. In both cases it can and must be said that the blockchain should not be seen as a technological solution but as a new, decentralized approach to the concept of trust.

An opposite view to the one that traditionally distinguishes the logic of verification and control in many human activities starting from the financial and economic ones, where a reliable and certified central "unit" is responsible for verifying and authorizing operations or transactions. With the blockchain, this verification and this authorization are not in a "center" but are in fact decentralized to all those who enter the chain with the role of blocks or nodes. It is a new concept of trust.


# Who Is Satoshi Nakamoto Really?

The blockchain seems to have been conceived by Satoshi Nakamoto (pseudonym of the inventor of the blockchain and its source code), and made famous by its best-known protocol, the virtual currency Bitcoin.

Satoshi Nakamoto revealed his project and vision in October 2008 with the publication of a white paper that talks and describes the possibility of developing a digital currency independent of any central body or institution in the form of Bitcoin. All with a code development path that Nakamoto started in 2007.

The white book called Bitcoin: a peer-to-peer electronic cash system immediately met with great interest, in particular because it opens up a perspective for monetary and financial exchanges in a decentralized form. The white paper was followed in January 2009 by the launch of the first Bitcoin software with the inauguration of the digital currency in the form of the first Bitcoin cryptocurrency unit in version 0.1 on the SourceForge development platform.

With that first important white paper, Nakamoto focuses attention on the core design of the blockchain model which appears capable or in the condition of supporting a large number of types of transactions. The white paper was then accompanied by the release of a website called bitcoin.org and promotes a development model based on collaboration with other developers.

# A Look at the History of Blockchain

The history of the blockchain begins in October 2008 when, as we have seen, Satoshi Nakamoto publishes the white paper Bitcoin: a peer-to-peer electronic cash system. Apparently, this is one of many white papers that illustrate the work and achievements of developers with both intuition and courage. But only apparently, because those who have had the opportunity to read behind the technical perspective of a digital currency, bitcoin to be precise, has seen much more than a brilliant technical-organizational intuition. Those who have read the white paper carefully and understood it have realized that it was a real revolution towards all forms of centralized organization, starting with banks. Bitcoin, or better still the Bitcoin blockchain, became a reality a few months later in January 2009 with the release of the first unit of Bitcoin cryptocurrency.

The Bitcoin blockchain immediately proved to work and in a short time the Bitcoin became the Blockchain, even if as we will correctly see Bitcoin is a blockchain and today there are many blockchains and they are also very different from each other.

In addition to becoming synonymous with blockchain, Bitcoin immediately became a political asset, thanks to the possibility of giving life to a relationship system, mostly financial, monetary, decentralized, distributed and ostentatiously democratic, thanks to attributes powerful as absolute transparency and immutability. With these characteristics in the womb and with the fact, not trivial, in the world of non-conventional development, that it works and works very well, blockchain technology has immediately become a political and ideological symbol. Moreover, the strong message launched by Satoshi Nakamoto is once again apparently technical and strongly political "We define digital coin as a chain of digital signatures": The Bitcoin blockchain is a chain of relationships based on trust. Trust is the key word to understand the blockchain.

The meaning of Satoshi Nakamoto's work is all here: in the relationships between two or more people who do not know each other and in this case in the relationships concerning a commercial transaction it is no longer necessary to refer to a third party, recognized by all as reliable. The transaction can be regulated among peers, by the network or by all the participants in the network, or better by the majority of the participants.

The third party, the center to which everyone recognizes a third role, that is of autonomous and independent and authoritative and reliable decision-making capacity, is no longer necessary. The system of relationships between the nodes of the network or between people can work.

The Bitcoin blockchain has shown that it is not necessary to have a central body to manage transactions.

For all those who have always contested the role of a central body, blockchain technology appeared as proof of the existence of an alternative model. Whether it was those who contested a centralized model regardless, that is, regardless of the quality of choices and behaviors, or whether it was those who contested a centralized vision of the world also on the merits of the behavior of those politically or in the economy or in other areas represented this "center", in any case the Blockchain has become a political symbol.

This is the first element to always consider, even when we will see the implications most closely linked to the business and pragmatically far from any political dimension.

Another reason that contributed to making the blockchain a non-ordinary phenomenon immediately is the mystery that still accompanies both Satoshi Nakamoto and some of the main "miners" who make the blockchain every day.

A mystery that in the case of Satoshi Nakamoto, for some a pseudonym that hides a group of developers who have been able to combine exceptional skills with a brilliant intuition and an ability to test and concretely demonstrate the feasibility of their project. Whatever the case, genius or geniuses, these are figures capable of opening a new chapter in the history of innovation and social issues.

## The Mathematical Problem of the Byzantine Generals

Let's stop for a moment at the concept of trust, because as we have seen it is the key to understanding the blockchain. The logic developed by Satoshi Nakamoto also arises from the resolution of a mathematical problem known as "the problem of the Byzantine generals". A sort of puzzle based on the need of a Byzantine general, during a siege, to send, through messengers, the order to attack the enemy to other lieutenants who are in different places.

The problem is that everyone knows that among them there are one or more traitors. How can each lieutenant be certain, once the attack order has been received, that the same order has been sent to the others as well? So, how can he be sure that he is not the only one to have received him in that form and therefore that all the other lieutenants are in a position to transmit and share the same order? How is it possible to guarantee the generals and all the lieutenants that no one tries to undermine the plan, or that if someone wants to try, he is not in a position to carry it out because everyone is effectively in a position to have the correct order?

The purpose of the problem, therefore, is to ensure that the correct plan of attack arrives to the honest lieutenants, without the traitors being able to compromise the operation by giving them the wrong information.

Up to now, the only possible answer to the question seemed to be the introduction of a trusted third party able to act as a guarantor of the authenticity of the order. Someone, with a reliability and authority recognized by everyone, to whom everyone could turn to verify the reliability of the information received.

But evidently, also for logistical reasons, this is an impractical solution in the case of the Byzantine generals problem. This eventual authoritative third party could not be reached by all the lieutenants.

Here the solution comes with the blockchain and it is a solution, which from a military point of view appears as a radical, indeed revolutionary, solution. The solution is to no longer have a "general" who commands over others. Therefore, there is no longer a center that prevails hierarchically. But the same hierarchy is assigned to all participants, or to be more precise, in the case of the blockchain, to all nodes. All the generals and all the lieutenants, i.e., all the nodes, participating in this model, agree on every single message transmitted between the nodes, see it and share it. That is, the network must agree on every message that is transmitted on the network itself. Everyone sees any message, and everyone sees any change to any part of the message and everyone can then also check the history, immutable, unchangeable and therefore incorruptible, of any previous step.

The message is then written in such a way as to be inaccessible and unchangeable by all those who are not part of the network or by all those who are not in the group of generals and lieutenants. That is, the messages are encrypted, and the access keys are available only and exclusively to all those who are part of the network. For all the others the message appears incomprehensible.

Any modification to the message, or indeed to the orders, can only be implemented with the consent mechanism, or by the majority of participants in the network and once a modification has been implemented, precisely through consent, even those who have not been able to participate (in the minority) can see exactly all the steps that led to that decision. The distributed consensus is not exactly in line with the principles of military strategy, but in the present case of the problem of the Byzantine generals it represents the solution to the issue of the presence of one or more traitors who can "corrupt" the correct knowledge and the correct dissemination of the orders established by generals. This way everyone knows everything in the exact same form.

The security of the blockchain is based on the nature and strength of distributed consensus.

Technology is superimposed on a sociological reading: archives or centralized networks, with a central computational capacity and therefore with a power and a "truth" managed by the center. On the contrary, we see a distributed model, where each one has its own computational capacity, as a node of the network, and each sees exactly the same truth that others see and has the same possibility (at least potentially) to contribute to changing it.

In between there is a hybrid situation called decentralized ledger and which maintains some specificities of centralized logic (i.e., a guiding role in terms of processing capacity and decision-making hierarchy) but no longer unique, i.e. together with other centers. It is on this decentralized dimension that the main business of the blockchain is developing.

## CHAPTER 3

# THE IMPORTANCE OF THE BLOCKCHAIN

Let's see concretely what the blockchain consists of. The blockchain is a communication protocol, which identifies a technology based on the logic of the distributed database (a database in which data is not stored on a single computer but on several connected machines, called nodes).

The blockchain is a series of blocks that store a set of transactions validated and correlated by a timestamp. Each block includes the hash (a non-invertible computer algorithmic function that maps a string of arbitrary length into a string of predefined length) which uniquely identifies the block and allows the connection with the previous block by identifying the previous block.

These below are the basic components of the blockchain:

- nodes: they are the participants in the blockchain and are physically constituted by the servers of each participant;
- transaction: it is made up of the data that represent the values subject to exchange and that need to be verified, approved and then archived;
- block: it is represented by the grouping of a set of transactions that are merged to be verified, approved and then archived by the participants in the blockchain;

- ledger: it is the public register in which all the transactions carried out in an orderly and sequential manner are recorded with the utmost transparency and in an immutable way. The Ledger consists of the set of blocks that are chained together through an encryption function and thanks to the use of hashes;
- hash: it is an operation that allows you to map a text and/or numeric string of variable length into a unique and univocal string of determined length. The Hash uniquely and securely identifies each block. A hash must not allow to trace the text that generated it.

Each block therefore contains several transactions and has a hash placed in the header. The hash records all the information relating to the block and a hash with the information relating to the previous block allows you to create the chain and link one block to the other.

The transaction instead contains information relating to the public address of the recipient, the characteristics of the transaction and the cryptographic signature that guarantees the security and authenticity of the transaction.

The blockchain is to be seen as a public and shared ledger made up of a series of clients or nodes.

The blockchain is organized to automatically update on each of the clients participating in the network. Each operation performed must be automatically confirmed by all individual nodes through cryptographic software, which verifies a packet of data defined as a private key or seed, which is used to sign the transactions. By guaranteeing the digital identity of those who authorized them.

As mentioned, the blockchain is a distributed database. So, to understand what blockchain is, it is necessary to better understand what a distributed database is, that is, a database, shared between multiple computers, called nodes, connected to the network.

# How Blockchain Works: an Example

In a simple way and with the iconographic support we see the steps that define the functioning of a transaction based on the blockchain.

The following example is about how to manage a transaction, an exchange or the sale of an asset with the blockchain.

Two parties have to make a transaction: for example, Paul sells a property to Hannah. The need arises to manage a commercial transaction between two parties.

The transaction with the cryptographic keys is created.

A transaction is created consisting of a series of elements such as the public address of the recipient, information relating to the transaction and the cryptographic keys. In the example of Paul and Hannah, the transaction includes information on the property, on the price, on Hannah's economic availability, on the actual ownership of the property by Paul and any other information necessary to complete the reference framework for the sale and for purchase.

In preparation for the transaction, Paul and Hannah's cryptographic keys are created. The transaction starts with each participant's digital signature and public key.

The transaction becomes part of a transaction block. A new block is created with all the data relating to the transaction between Paul and Hannah and with the data relating to the property and Paul's financial resources. The block, which also includes other transactions, is prepared to be subjected to verification and approval by the participants in the blockchain.

The transaction between Paul and Hannah becomes part of a block that will be verified and solved by the participants in the blockchain.

The Block, with the transaction, must be verified by the network. The transaction is brought online to be verified by the participants in the blockchain.

The block that includes the transaction between Paul and Hannah, together with other transactions, is verified and approved by the blockchain network.

Once verified, the block is added to the chain: here is the blockchain.

The new block is added to the block chain that forms the blockchain, is accessible to all participants and is in the archive of all participants. It becomes the permanent, immutable and unchangeable reference of that specific transaction.

The Block which also includes the transaction between Paul and Hannah is added to the blockchain and becomes part of the "chain" of blocks.

The transaction is completed and is stored on all nodes of the blockchain. If the information is considered correct, the transaction is authorized, validated and carried out. At that point, the transaction becomes part of a new block that is created, and which also includes this transaction.

The transaction between Paul and Hannah is published on the blockchain and is accessible to all participants and no one will be able to modify it. The transaction in all its components is and remains immutable over time.

# What Is a Distributed Database?

Let's take a step back to better understand what a distributed database is. When we talk about distributed ledger, we are faced with a database that is not physically located only on a server, but which is instead located on several computers at the same time, all perfectly synchronized on all the same documents. For example, it can be on all computers that are connected to the network. In this way, information can be found very quickly, as the computing power uses the power of all connected computers.

There are basically two processes that allow distributed databases to function properly, and not to lose data along the way. These processes are:
- database replication: a software is in charge of analyzing the database to identify changes. Once these changes are identified, the software ensures that these changes are replicated and that all databases are identical;
- duplication: a process that ensures that all databases have the same data. In practice, it identifies a master database, which it then duplicates on all the other databases, in order to make them the same. Users can only modify the master database, ensuring that local data is not mistakenly overwritten.

Becoming famous because of Bitcoins, the blockchain is essentially a distributed database, where a series of records, called blocks, are recorded.

## CHAPTER 4

# DISTRIBUTED LEDGER TECHNOLOGY - DLT

The Ledger is the fundamental basis of accounting. Ledgers then refer to archives, or rather to a series of data that allow you to define rules of analysis, control, verification, for example, of the commercial transactions of a company or of the acts of a Public Administration.

Until the advent of computerization, ledgers were interpreted with the centralized logic that characterized paper. There was someone who took care of the data entry of data that originated as analog, there was someone who managed the systems and there was someone who centrally managed the data extraction or their processing.

In the first phase of computerization, digitalization has not actually changed the processes, it has made them more efficient in compliance with an analog process: it has speeded up some steps and simplified certain checks and verifications. But the data continued to be conceived as analog and managed with an analog paradigm, albeit with digital tools. Just think of the "iron" logic that requires for the vast majority of documents that punctuate our personal and professional life the need for a paper signature and physical and personal control by administrations or companies.

How does a blockchain-type distributed ledger system work?

In order to explain how blockchain-type distributed ledgers

work, it may be useful to refresh your mind on how traditional ledgers work, or rather the "old ledgers".

# How Old Ledgers Work

Companies, but above all banks and public administrations have used ledgers to manage accounting and archiving of data and accounting transactions. The public administrations, in turn, have based the registrations and transfers of properties for land, buildings and real estate assets on ledgers.

With each change, for example in the ownership of a property and each time a transaction took place, the ledger was changed through a central authority responsible for managing the central ledger. With this organization, by acting on the central ledger, the offices of public administrations or credit institutions could at any time know and identify the owner of a property or certain resources. This control allowed the banks themselves or public offices to verify that any steps related to new transactions on certain assets were actually possible and above all legitimate. In other words, with the central ledger it was possible to verify whether the subject X in the process of selling the property Y was actually in possession of that property or had not already sold it to a subject Z. The bank, in turn, could check that subject H about to purchase property Y from subject X was actually in possession of the necessary sum and had not already used it for other acquisitions, or that the same sum was not used for multiple operations.

# The Basis of the Central Ledger Is All About Trust in a Central Body

The basis of the central ledger is all enclosed in the trust that everyone, indeed, must have in the central ledger manager. Banks and public administrations must have that authority capable of instilling this confidence. If there is this trust, people can buy and sell even without having ever met before and in the absence of mutual trust. Because there is a third party that guarantees for everyone. The manager of the ledger also controls access to the information contained in the ledger and has the right to decide who can access the identity of the owner of a building and who can check the balance of a current account. All this by defining the rules that make up an overall design of guidelines that establish the governance of the central ledger.

In the case of banks, only current account holders have access and visibility of their current account. But when these owners are engaged in the purchase of an asset (for example a property) it is the bank that guarantees, during the acquisition procedures, that these subjects actually have the sum necessary for the acquisition without other subjects having access to their bank account.

## Digitization has changed ledgers

With digitization, this process has undergone evolutions and accelerations. Digitization has changed ledgers, like so many other elements of our professional and personal life, but ledgers have undergone a radical change, well before other work tools.

In a first phase, digitization made ledger faster, easier to use, more performing and allowed to add many features. However, digitization has not changed the logic of the ledger. The old central ledger hasn't been questioned. The ledgers remained in the hands of a central structure that took advantage of digital opportunities for management and, above all, remained closed and reserved. Governance has not changed, the rules of access and management remained with the central manager of the ledger, even when the relationship with this manager, exploiting the opportunities of digital, ceased to be personal and physical and became virtual by passing on the Internet.

# Big Change Comes With the Blockchain

The Great change comes with blockchain, which allows to guarantee the same functionality in the management of ledgers, but without having to refer to a centralized structure, that is, without the need for a central authority to verify, control and authorize the legitimacy of a transaction, of an exchange, of a passage.

The question that arises is: how can the legitimacy of a transaction be verified if there is no central authority that has the ability to carry out the necessary checks? The answer of the blockchain is in the decentralization of the ledger.

If before the ledger was unique, only one and was in the head of the central authority, now the ledger belongs to everyone, i.e., all users have a copy of it and everyone can check it, view it and, in the face of rules that go to compose the governance of the blockchain, they can modify it.

# Ledger Belongs to Everyone

So, the first real big step between the management of traditional ledgers and the blockchain is given by the fact that the ledgers are many and that they are accessible to everyone. The second big step is that everyone can implement a transaction or modify an existing one. In both cases, this request can only be implemented if all (or most users) agree to implement it. And the fact that they are all, most or a certain number of subjects with certain characteristics, once again introduces us to the rules that define the governance of the blockchain. Regardless, however, whether the transaction is authorized by all or by a certain number of participants, the transaction request will certainly be accepted only if the participants agree on its legitimacy. This verification is allowed by the fact that all participants can check that the request comes from a person authorized to carry it out. To return to the previous example, everyone is invited to check that the seller of the property Y is actually the owner and has not sold the property. At the same time, everyone is invited to check that those who are preparing to buy the property actually have the necessary amount and have not already used it for other purchases.

Now the question is: how does this check happen? Is it possible that all participants have to carry out personal checks on each transaction? With the blockchain, these checks are performed reliably and automatically on behalf of each user. Each operation contributes to creating a quick and safe ledger system which, by being distributed to all participants (all participants have a copy of each operation), is also able to resist any tampering.

# The Great Ledger of the Blockchain

Let's get back to transactions. Each new transaction to be recorded is combined with other new transactions and forms a block, which is added as a link in a long chain of historical transactions. Each time a block is generated, the chain is lengthened. This chain makes up the great blockchain ledger which is owned by all users.

# The Role of the Miners

For a new block of transactions to be added to the blockchain, it must be checked, validated and encrypted. Only with this step it can then become active and be added to the blockchain. To carry out this step, it is necessary that every time a block is composed a complex mathematical problem is solved which requires a conspicuous commitment also in terms of power and processing capacity. This operation is defined as "mining" and is carried out by "miners".
The work of the miner is absolutely fundamental in the economics of blockchain management. Anyone can become a miner and can compete to be the first to solve the complex mathematical problem of creating each new block of transactions in a valid and encrypted way that can be added to the blockchain.

### Bitcoin mining at the basis of the functioning of the blockchain

Since this is an important commitment, as mentioned with a considerable expenditure of energy, cryptocurrency mining is a commitment that needs to be remunerated and incentivized. In private or permissioned blockchains, this role is played, depending on governance, by the authority that activates the blockchain itself.

In public or permissionless blockchains, this role can be played by any participant in the blockchain, and the miner is incentivized with forms of remuneration that depend on the type of rules or governance defined by each blockchain.

In most cases, the first miner who creates a valid block and adds it to the chain is rewarded with the sum of their transaction fees. The commissions refer to unit values for each single transaction, but the blocks are added regularly and can contain thousands of transactions, so the value of the miner can also be very significant. Miners can also receive new currencies created and put into circulation as an inflation mechanism, such as in the case of the Bitcoin blockchain.

But let's go back to the ledger. The operation that adds a new block to the chain updates the ledger held by all participants in the blockchain. These participants therefore accept a new block when - thanks to the solution of the complex mathematical problem - the validity of all its transactions has been verified.

In the event that the verification process detects an error, an anomaly, a discrepancy, the block is rejected, and everyone has visibility of the fact that the transaction was not authorized. Otherwise, if all transactions are validated, the block is created and added and will become part of the blockchain in effect as a permanent and immutable public record; no participant in the blockchain will be able to change or remove it.

# Immutability of the Blockchain

Immutability is the other great value of the blockchain which obviously also relates to data security. If we go back to the example of the "old" ledger we must remember that to change or damage or destroy a central ledger - it is necessary to violate the central authority that manages it, in the case of the blockchain it is impossible because it would be necessary to breach all copies of the ledger owned by all participants of the blockchain and it would have to be done simultaneously.

An operation that is practically impossible, although obviously it is necessary to evaluate the size of the blockchain in terms of participants or nodes. At the same time, there cannot even be a fake ledger as all participants have a single authentic version that they can challenge for comparison and verification. Here we come to the concept of trust and control. Trust and control of transactions pass from the central authority to all participants. Transactions based on the blockchain are not centralized and hidden or "closed", but they are decentralized and transparent, open to everyone.

In this case, the blockchain is of the permissionless type, that is without authorizations and there is no special authority that can deny authorization to participate in the control and addition of transactions.

Blockchains that require authorizations are defined as permissioned and define governance that assigns management and authority to define access, controls, authorizations and above all the ability to add transactions to the ledger to a specific group of operators. Permissioned blockchains can combine the values of transparency, immutability and security of blockchains, guaranteeing certain subjects such as banks, companies and public administrations the possibility of a control, even significant and substantial, on the methods of execution of transactions.

## From ledgers to distributed ledgers thanks to the blockchain

Let's see how we get to the blockchain. From the first digital ledgers there has been an acceleration in terms of innovation thanks to the simultaneous availability of three enabling factors: cryptography, the development of data control and verification algorithms that open the doors to those who become distributed ledger technology.

With distributed ledger technology you enter the field of distributed databases, or ledgers that can be updated, managed, controlled and coordinated no longer only centrally, but in a distributed way, by all the players.

The prerequisites for distributed ledger technology are in the creation of large networks made up of a series of participants and each participant is called upon to manage a node of this network. Each node is authorized to update the distributed ledger independently from the others but under the consensual control of the other nodes.

Updates or records are no longer managed, as was traditionally the case, under the strict control of a central authority, but are instead created and loaded by each node independently. In this way, each participant is able to process and check each transaction but at the same time each individual transaction, even if managed independently, must be verified, voted and approved by the majority of the network participants. And here we come to the basis of the concept of distributed ledger technology or the concept of consensus. The autonomy of each node is subject to the achievement of a consensus on the operations that are carried out and only with this consent are they then authorized and activated.


# DLT: Centrality Lies in the Consensus Rule

Distributed ledgers are updated only after obtaining consent and each node is updated with the latest version of each individual operation of each participant. Each operation then remains indelibly and immutable on each single node.

In other words, each participant has an immutable copy of each operation. As you can see, this is a nice change from traditional centralized logic, when verification and authorization were centralized and when the same access to all archives was managed centrally.

This architecture model allows to interpret the database in a much broader sense than in the past. We can no longer simply speak of ledger as archives, but we must speak of distributed ledger technology as a new relationship between people and information.


**Algorithms and peer-to-peer network at the base of DLT**
Distributed ledger technologies, which are also known as shared ledgers, need a peer-to-peer network and algorithms capable of managing the collection of consent and the approval of operations based precisely on the achievement of a consensus.

It is the consensus management models that determine the difference between public and private distributed ledger technology.

However, it should be noted that not necessarily all distributed ledgers refer to blockchains for the purpose of managing consensus.
Blockchain is one of several consensus management possibilities used to apply distributed ledger technology.

## CHAPTER 5

# BLOCKCHAIN SECURITY

One of the most important features of the blockchain is security. The time stamp also prevents the operation, once performed, from being altered or canceled.

The main feature of the model, therefore, is that its operation is not guaranteed by a central body, but each individual transaction is validated by the interaction of all nodes.

The time stamp allows you to associate a certain and legally valid date and time with an IT document. In other words, the time stamp allows you to define a temporal validation that can be opposed to third parties.

## What Is a Time Stamp?

The time stamp consists of a specific sequence of characters that uniquely, indelibly and immutably identify a date and/or time to fix and ascertain the actual occurrence of a certain event. The representation of the date is developed in a format that allows it to be compared with other dates and allows you to establish and define a temporal order. The practice of applying this time stamp is called timestamping.

But what is timestamping? The application of the time stamp is a process that is defined as timestamping and is one of the operating bases of the blockchain.

# What Is the Distributed Consensus?

The blockchain validation process involves a verification and approval phase based on computing resources that are made available by the participants in the blockchain and which are aimed at solving complex problems or cryptographic puzzles and which allow for a no more than a consent based on a third-party intermediary or a centralized body or institution.

Those who participate in the resolution of the problem and therefore contribute to the validation of the process and the transaction are called miners, and their intervention, which requires important resources to be carried out, is remunerated through the issuance of a virtual currency or cryptocurrency.

The logic behind this process starts from the assumption that in order to avoid the risk of fraud in particular by a node of the blockchain it is necessary to create obstacles and complications throughout the validation process. Specifically, each node intending to participate in validation must also solve a complex problem in the form of a cryptographic puzzle. The puzzle is designed to put all nodes in competition, and all contribute to the resolution by making their computing power available. The node that will be able to solve the cryptographic puzzle will have the right to validate the block with the presentation of the proof of labor which is also the proof of the solution of the puzzle. For this commitment and for this result, the node is in fact remunerated with a unit of value that depends on the type of blockchain.

It should then be added that in blockchains the nodes are not public, that is, they do not know each other, and the proof of labor also represents the way to build a relationship of trust based on concrete collaboration in solving the tests that must be validated.

# The Heart of the Blockchain

Digital currencies do not come with the blockchain, there have been experiments and digital transaction projects with digital coins and there are many, since well before the arrival of Satoshi Nakamoto's white paper. In many respects also very positive and significant. However, all the projects carried out clashed with the unsolved problem of double spending, the most difficult test.

**What is double spending?**
Digital is by definition infinitely duplicable at marginal costs. To be clear, digital has opened the era of the intangible economy and has its foundations precisely on the ability to make a good or service (a software, a piece of music, an eBook) available to both a customer and millions of customers exactly in the same identical form at infinitely lower marginal costs than the logic of the material world.
An amazing opportunity that, as is well known, has changed entire industries and is at the root of the phenomenon of digital transformation, but also a non-trivial limit when you want to be sure that a certain asset is not then duplicated outside certain business or ethical rules. If you duplicate a piece of music or an application you enter an order of problems that have long been the subject of debate, such as ethics and business.
If you then duplicate a currency, or if, with the same currency, you have the possibility to pay two or more times for different goods, it is clear that this is a problem that undermines any type of commercial relationship.
Double spending is intended as a guarantee that the same digital monetary asset cannot be used multiple times for multiple purchases, like any other currency that "changing

hands" explicitly with this step the transfer of a value in exchange for merchandise or service. In traditional digital currency, this task is entrusted to the banks that deal with reconciling the transfer of value from our account to that of those who sold us an asset with more or less complex steps depending on the type of payment service that we used. In the context of "pure digital", the double spending problem was addressed with solutions that worked on tracking issues and that achieved certain objectives but exposed to certain risks.

**The double spending solution with the Bitcoin blockchain**
The resolution of double spending, or the ability to prevent a coin from being used twice by the same person both to buy a meal and to buy a trip, is one of the great insights present in Satoshi Nakamoto's white book.
The resolution is essentially in the identity of the currency. The cryptography that accompanies bitcoin and in general the different declinations of the blockchain allow you to manage the identity of the cryptocurrency, with its specific ID code, its name and surname and its history. Example: Philip buys a meal with coin A (ID: 754490). The transaction archives the passage of coin A from Philip's wallet to Paul's in exchange for an asset. All the nodes of the blockchain, all the participants, will be informed of this transaction. But the coin itself, A, will add in his resume, which served to pay for a clearly identified asset of a clearly identified person given to a clearly identified person. The same coin A (ID: 754490) will be enriched with information when Paul uses it for other transactions and when the beneficiary of this new transaction in turn uses it for a new purchase. Philip will no longer have access to coin A (ID: 754490) and will not even have a copy of that coin.

## The resolution of double spending

Philip buys a service from Paul and a good from Hannah. Philip owns a clearly identified asset.

Philip pays Paul for the good he has purchased and at the same time the currency changes and in turn changes ownership, maintaining his identity and uniqueness and putting the transaction data on file.

The purchase with Paul can be made with a new currency, with a new ID in turn unique that allows Philip to transfer a unique and secure value to Paul.

It is as if the banknotes we have in our wallet, or those we have in our online current account, or those that are in the app managed by our wallets, could talk and could tell the whole story of the transactions they made possible.

In spite of the criticisms that accompanied a first phase of the Bitcoin blockchain accused of being used as a platform for illegal payments or financing, it is clear that, once the great issue of the identity of the blockchain participants (i.e. that Philip, Paul and Hannah are actually Philip, Paul and Hannah registered with their names, surnames and all the data that define and determine our identity), the Bitcoin blockchain rather than other cryptocurrencies are the most traceable and secure there can be.

But what if it is the participants of the blockchain who attempt a double spending? Since each node contains the same information as the others and, in this way, knows the entire history of the transactions that have taken place, as well as all the other nodes, how can you be sure that blocks containing false transactions are not validated?

If there was a node that, surreptitiously, tried (and succeeded, but it must be said that it is extremely difficult) to alter the history of transactions, inserting a false transaction such as to generate a problem about the ownership (or rather about the transfer of ownership) of the traded asset, one would run into a situation of double spending.

It could be that the asset transferred from Paul to Philip is, an instant after the transfer from Paul, re-attributed to Paul, thanks to the intervention of a node that voluntarily changes (in this case to the detriment of Philip) history of that transaction. Only when, perhaps even after a long time, Philip tries to transfer the asset that he believes of him to others, he will realize that it is not actually his property. To understand how unlikely and difficult this eventuality is, let's briefly see the steps that determine this type of transaction.

The exchange in Cryptocurrency units is also based on reading and checking the list of transactions carried out up to the moment in which the new transaction takes place, which in our example corresponds to a transfer of ownership of an asset. The proof of the passage of the new ownership is created thanks to a digital signature of the transaction itself by the last person who exchanged cryptocurrency related to this transaction. The passage of cryptocurrencies from Paul to Philip are fixed through a timestamp service that compresses the block, together with the transfer of ownership of the asset "paid for" with the cryptocurrencies. The block is precisely stamped and published with compression (hash). Each timestamp in turn includes the previous one in its hash, forming a chain (the blockchain) which is then public and shared. With these conditions, it becomes extremely difficult to alter all the components of a transaction, that is, to create the conditions for a double spending situation to occur.

If we then replace the concept of curriculum associated with a currency with the curriculum associated with the history of a raw material, for example in the world of fashion or food, one can imagine what extraordinary potential this opens up. The grape that can tell its entire story, from the moment it is picked to the moment it arrives on the restaurant table or on the retailer's shelf. And if you think that all those who participate in the blockchain can see it and that the story, once approved is immutable and accessible to all, one realizes that we are facing a technology that not only leads to a change in performance, but a paradigm shift. The blockchain solves not only double spending but a whole series of issues related to unique and secure identity.

It is no coincidence that it is said that the blockchain is the new Internet, to be precise it is said that from the Internet of information we pass to the Internet of values and transactions.

# Tokens: What They Are and How They Work

A token is a blockchain-based digital asset that can be exchanged between two parties without the need for the action of an intermediary. A token can be seen as a set of digital information that is able to confer a property right to a subject over the same set of information that is recorded on a blockchain and that can be transferred via a protocol.

The token can possibly also incorporate other additional rights which in the case are governed by a system of smart contracts. One of the first examples of tokens is represented by Bitcoin, but in a short time many others have appeared, some starting from the experience of Bitcoin itself, others using new models and new code such as the Ethereum blockchain. The tokens created thanks to Ethereum have different attributes that allow the management of smart contracts, in order to establish the agreement between the parties in an increasingly binding and secure manner.

**An example to understand how tokens work**
To understand what tokens are and how they work, you can use the example of payphone tokens. The telephone tokens were used to obtain a very concrete service: the telephone call from public booths.
The coin was a token and had a value of 1 dollar. In an ICO, in some respects, a token is issued that is used to use a service. In this way the company obtains resources that it can use without contracting any obligation towards those who made the investments (unlike IPOs, where there are of course obligations) other than to make the service available to those who will be ready to pay for it with their own token, or by spending the value asset that they purchased during the ICO phase.
The old payphone coin like the token can be exchanged due to its intrinsic value. A payphone token had a recognized value of 1 dollar which the shopkeepers accepted because they were certain of putting that coin back into circulation which was in fact a valuable asset. Therefore, the token created for the provision of a service (the telephone call from public booths) had become an asset also used for the management of small transactions.
If the company that owns the service and protagonist of the issue legitimately decided that the value of the phone call was no longer comparable to a token of 1 dollar but to a value of 2 dollars and consequently increased the value of the token, here is that whoever had purchased a certain number of tokens (not for an investment but in anticipation of making many phone calls) was found to have the same value in terms of quantity of telephone services, but a doubled value in terms of valuable assets to be used on the market as an exchange currency.

The ICO token is a bit like the payphone token. If the issuer promises to provide a service that can be purchased thanks to the token, he finds himself with an investment made by subjects who intend to use that service or who believe in the value of that service to the point of acquiring many tokens to use it or to sell them to others who will be able to use them. If there are no services behind the token, the risk is that it is just a new form of investment. Here it appears very important to carefully analyze all the various forms of tokens.

## Different Types of Tokens

There are different types of tokens determined both by the type of technological approach and by the type of use.
In particular, it is important to focus attention on three different types of tokens determined by the type of rights managed by the tokens themselves:

- CLASS 1 TOKEN: the token looks like a real coin, has no counterparty and can be transferred via blockchain transactions. The token is also a guarantee of the non-modifiability of the transactions themselves. It is a type of token that does not confer rights on a counterpart, but has the function of registering a right of ownership of the token itself or the existence of a specific subject/object. With this type of token, the owner has no further rights than those related to ownership of the token itself. The tokens of cryptocurrencies such as Bitcoin, Bitcoin Cash, Litecoin, and so on, are part of the category of Class 1 tokens;

- CLASS 2 TOKENS: in this case they are tokens that are able to give the owners the rights that can be exercised against the person who generated the tokens or possibly against third parties. These are tokens that therefore allow you to exercise rights towards counterparties. In different words, it could be said that class 2 tokens could be defined as a sort of credit instruments, or rather documents which confer on the holder the right to the service indicated therein towards presentation of the title. As in everyday life, these can be bonds or loan securities, participation securities, securities representing goods and documents of legitimation. But to better understand what this really means, we cite the examples of the following types of class 2 tokens;

1. tokens for smart contracts relating to the management of future payments: with the granting of a right to receive future payments, on the basis of certain contractual conditions that the token is required to manage in an automatic way;
2. token as an asset: in this case the token represents a sort of ownership right of a given asset (both tangible and intangible) and for example it could also represent stakes of the issuing legal entity or third party entities;
3. tokens used for standardized payments: where a person has the right to receive a payment for a specific, well-defined amount;
4. token for the management of the provision of services: in this circumstance the holder of the token has the right to receive a specific service or in the case also a good from the issuer or from a third party who has signed a commercial agreement. For example, these are tokens that regulate access to IT infrastructures, the provision of

services and which may also have the characteristics of a native cryptocurrency;

- CLASS 3 TOKENS: these are tokens that can perform a mixed function. They are tokens that represent co-ownership rights or that represent a property but also confer different rights, such as the right to vote, or economic rights for legal representatives or shareholders of a company, etc. In this type of token, the holder does not have a right that can be exercised directly towards the issuer of the security or towards a third party.

# Tokenization

Alongside Tokenization, a modality defined as Tokenization based on the so-called "labeled tokens" has also developed. The issue and management of "labeled tokens" (LB) or token+ is a procedure that associates a series of metadata to the tokens for which the exchange is conducted on a secondary market, through smart contracts on the Ethereum blockchain.

Tokenization+ is an evolution of both the ICO and the ITO (Initial Coin Offering, Initial Token Offering) and is used in many international projects.

**What are the advantages of token+**
Compared to the traditional token, the token+ has five great advantages:
- it is individually and uniquely labeled and has associated metadata;
- it is not divisible;
- exists in digital form on the blockchain;

- it can also be followed individually in its path/history of chain of ownership;
- it can be managed in different ways for each label according to the meaning/value of the metadata.

## Where Tokenization+ is used

Tokenization+ can be used as a financing tool in the various phases of business development, from seed to series C/tech growth and can also be used as an alternative or alongside other instruments such as VC, Stock Market, Business Angel, Funds, Banks.

In particular, Tokenization+ can be addressed to four specific areas, where the management of smart conctracts is not in contrast with the provisions of the current jurisdiction:

- innovative business projects based on blockchain;
- innovative business projects not based on blockchain;
- non-innovative business projects;
- tangible assets (real estate, works of art, etc.) or intangible assets and services (such as software, families of collectible digital elements) of any nature.

It must be said, that exactly as for the 'traditional' coin/tokens in the various countries, analyzes and studies are currently underway to define the regulation to be applied case by case, also for token+ a similar phase of examination is necessary, to understand what are the advantages related to the presence of the label, i.e. the label, and how to use the metadata in compliance with the rules on privacy, investor or consumer protection, anti-money laundering, identity (KYC).

## CHAPTER 6

# OPERATING LOGICS OF THE BLOCKCHAIN

The model is based on the combination of digital signature and time stamp: the first guarantees that the sender and recipient of any type of message (for example the transaction in the world of payments) are identified in a certain set of messages, validated with the time stamp by a node chosen randomly from a robust mathematical model, is communicated and written in the register of all the other nodes in the network and made irreversible.

All operations, in the case of Bitcoin, are confirmed by the network within ten minutes (but faster protocols have also been developed, such as that of Litecoin), through the distributed consensus process known as mining. In practice, the correctness of the block of operations entered into the network is verified by the computers of the network participants by comparing it with the most updated version of the blockchain. The first node that gets a green light communicates it to all the others, who validate the block by updating the blockchain. In this way, the chronological order of operations and net neutrality are preserved at the same time.

# Main Features of the Blockchain

What are the main features of the blockchain? Let's see them together.

Reliability
The blockchain is reliable. Not being governed by the center, but by giving all direct participants a part of control of the entire chain, the blockchain becomes a less centralized system, less governable, and at the same time much more secure and reliable, for example from malicious attacks.
In fact, if only one of the nodes in the chain is attacked and damaged, all the other nodes of the distributed database will still continue to be active and operational, welding the chain and thus not losing important information.

Transparency
Transactions made through the blockchain are visible to all participants, thus ensuring transparency in operations.

Convenience
Carrying out transactions through the blockchain is convenient for all participants, as there are fewer third-party interlocutors, necessary in all conventional transactions that take place between two or more parties (i.e., banks and other similar entities).

Solidity
The information already entered in the blockchain cannot be changed in any way. In this way the information contained in the blockchain is all more solid and reliable, precisely due to the fact that it cannot be altered and therefore remains as it was entered the first time.

## Irrevocability

With the blockchain it is possible to carry out irrevocable transactions, and at the same time more easily traceable. This ensures that transactions are final, with no possibility of being changed or canceled.

## Digitality

With the blockchain everything becomes virtual. Thanks to digitization, the fields of application of this new technology become many.


# Permissionless or Permissioned Ledger

To better understand the areas of use of distributed ledger technology, it is also necessary to know permissionless ledger (public blockchain) and permissioned ledger (private blockchain).

The permissionless ledgers, of which the most famous and widespread example is represented by the Bitcoin blockchain, are open, do not have a property or a reference actor and are designed not to be controlled.

The objective of the permissionless ledger is to allow everyone to contribute to the updating of data on the ledger and to have, as a participant, all the immutable copies of all operations. That is, to have all identical copies of everything that is approved thanks to consent.

This blockchain model prevents any form of censorship, no one is in a position to prevent a transaction from taking place and from being added to the ledger once it has won the necessary consensus among all the nodes (participants) of the blockchain.

Permissionless ledgers can be used as a global database for all those documents that need to be absolutely immutable over time unless updates require maximum security in terms of consent, such as property contracts or wills.

Closer to the needs of companies, permissioned ledgers can instead be controlled and therefore can have a property. When a new data or record is added, the approval system is not tied to the majority of participants in the blockchain but to a limited number of actors who can be defined as trusted.

This type of blockchain can be used by institutions, large companies that have to manage supply chains with a series of actors, companies that have to manage suppliers and sub-suppliers, banks, service companies, operators in the retail sector. In this case, the permissioned ledgers respond to the need for a widespread update on several actors who can operate independently, but with limited control to those who are authorized. The permissioned ledger then allows you to define special rules for access and visibility of all data.

In other words, the permissioned ledgers introduce a concept of governance and the definition of rules of behavior into the blockchain.

Technically, the permissioned ledger is even more performing and faster than the permissionless ledger.

When we started talking about smart contracts or intelligent contracts, the first thought and the first simplification was to consider them as a threat to the work of lawyers and notaries. But it is not at all true that the blockchain or rather, one of the dimensions of the blockchain such as smart contracts are destined to question the work of law firms or notaries. Certainly, like all transformations, it will impose a change, and certainly these professionals will be asked to review their role in the creation of highly innovative contractual forms.

But to understand what kind of change will come or is coming with smart contracts and which sectors will be before others interested it is important to understand what it is.

# Fundamental Elements for the Implementation of Private or Permissioned Blockchains

In private or permissioned blockchains, four major elements are valid: infrastructure, ecosystem, applications, and governance.

## The role of infrastructure in the private or permissioned blockchain

Private blockchains must be able to rely on reliable and extensively tested private or closed networks. The security of these solutions is directly linked to the ability to guarantee the impenetrability of the network by subjects who are not authorized. The infrastructure consists of networks and nodes.

## An ecosystem for private blockchains

Private or permissioned blockchains are populated by a series of actors who must strictly share the same values and rules. The principle also applies to companies that are called upon to provide private blockchain services both at the infrastructure, application development and service level.

All the actors are called to create an ecosystem, or to share the governance rules in all the planning, development and management activities of the private blockchain, which must then be implemented with the companies that will use the blockchain.

**The development of applications for private blockchains**
Development companies, software houses, system integrators or application providers who create solutions for private blockchains are called upon to work in the form of strictly close and controlled partnerships with infrastructure providers. The application component in private blockchains is closely linked to the technological and governance logic defined by companies to focus on the infrastructure.

**Governance in private blockchains**
The private or permissioned blockchain is based first and foremost on a set of rules shared by all the players. The rules are part of the development itself and to implement a private blockchain it is necessary to work in the conception and design phase both on the infrastructure and on the application logic. Governance is an integral part of the design process and represents the basis on which the production activities are then implemented as a set of rules that allow, first of all, to guarantee the absolute security of the blockchain for all actors and of course the achievement of the objectives of business of the companies and organizations that will be called upon to use it.

# Fork

Forks are tools used by the blockchain network to improve the performance of the blockchain and to manage the protocol. They are divided into soft fork and hard fork.

## Soft fork

The soft fork is created and implemented giving life to an updated version of the blockchain protocol compatible with previous versions. The soft fork implements a reversible change that allows participation in the blockchain network also to all those nodes that for various reasons decide not to upgrade.

## Hard fork

The hard fork foresees an irreversible change and requires blockchain participants to compulsorily upgrade. With the hard forks, new cryptocurrencies are created as for example in the past the cases of Bitcoin cash or before that Zcash and Litecoin.

## Planned or contentious hard fork

Hard forks can be planned, meaning planned and scheduled, or contentious, meaning they can't find community consensus.

In the case of the contentious hard forks, the proposed change to the protocol does not find an agreement within the community and with the hard fork we arrive at a form of splitting the blockchain. The contentious hard fork lead to the creation of a new currency.

In the case of planned hard fork the protocol change is planned and the change is approved by the community participants. The planned hard fork does not lead to the splitting of the blockchain, and the rules are updated in the form of continuity.

But why do we get to a fork? The reasons that can lead to a hard fork are different but can be summarized in a few of the following points.

## The scalability of the blockchain network

One of the themes that leads the community of blockchain participants to face a fork is that of scalability. For example, in the case of the blockchain network, the starting point is a blockchain created to process transactions every ten minutes. A time closely related to the amount of transactions and the number of participants. In the second half of 2017 there was an exponential increase in registrations due to a very strong increase in the diffusion of the currency. This demand has also translated into a slowdown in the time of processing consolidation of blocks on the blockchain. And we come to the forks or the theme of the division between the family of developers who on the one hand wish to maintain the traditional structure of the blockchain and developers who, on the other hand, wish to increase the volume of blocks and transactions, thus trying to make registrations faster.

This contrast has generated some forks of the blockchain and the birth of new virtual currencies originating from the Bitcoin blockchain (such as Bitcoin Cash and Bitcoin Gold).

## Risk of weakening the trust

It must not be forgotten that each new separation of the blockchain also determines the risk of a possible centralization in the management of the blockchain itself and therefore of weakening of the trust mechanism, i.e., a trust that is directly proportional to the number of participants in the blockchain.

## Ensure democratic management of the blockchain

If we start from the assumption that, for miners, the probabilities of winning the proof of labor are directly proportional to the computing capacity available, we note that the Bitcoin blockchain is exposed to a risk of imbalance in favor of those who can dispose of it of greater computing power or, in other respects, can access greater computing capacity at more accessible costs. In these cases, the corrective interventions have for example the purpose of defining innovations at the protocol level that make it possible to lower the weight of the importance of calculation capacity in the resolution of proof of work or trying to reduce the risk of concentration of miners.

## Improve performance and scalability
The theme of performance and scalability has always accompanied the development of the blockchain. The ability to process Bitcoin transactions compares with time limits of the order of less than 10 transactions per second. One of the themes of the community is precisely that of having a protocol that can improve these performances. One of the ways is to increase the size of the block, or to double the amount of transactions present in each block.

## Improve the governance of the network
The interventions on the blockchain protocol also have the purpose of managing the blockchain ecosystem or the set of rules and balances that underlie the view of the blockchain itself. One of the themes is in the very management of the forks and, to be precise, the hard forks which, bringing the community to face real splits, poses a theme of protection of the overall value of the ecosystem and, directly, also a theme of shared rules, of distributed and shared governance for Bitcoin.

# Smart Contract and Blockchain

Smart contracts were the subject of experimentation as early as the 90s when technologies made it possible to implement forms of smart contract experimentation, but the idea of the smart contract actually dates back to the mid-70s. At the time, the need was very simple and related to the need to manage the activation or deactivation of a software license according to some very simple conditions. The license of certain software was in fact managed by a digital key that allowed the software to function if the customer had paid for the license and ceased its operation on the expiry date of the contract.

**An automatic contract that is activated under certain conditions**
The smart contract needs legal support for its drafting, but it does not need it for its verification and activation. The smart contract refers to standards of behavior and access to certain services and is made available, accepted and implemented also as a form of development of traditional services. A smart contract is the translation or transposition of a contract into code in order to automatically verify the fulfillment of certain conditions (control of basic data of the contract) and to automatically carry out actions (or provide instructions for can perform certain actions) when the conditions determined between the parties are met and verified. In other words, the smart contract is based on a code that reads both the clauses that have been agreed and the operating conditions in which the agreed conditions must occur and automatically executes itself when the data referring to real situations correspond to the data referred to the agreed conditions and clauses.

**Why smart contracts need big data and data science**
Precisely because the absence of human intervention also corresponds to the absence of an interpretative contribution, the smart contract must be based on extremely precise descriptions for all circumstances, all conditions and all situations that must be considered. Here the management of data and big data in particular becomes an essential critical factor to establish the quality of the smart contract.

At the same time, for smart contracts it is essential to define in an extremely precise way the data sources to which the contract is required to comply. Smart contracts are required to receive data and information from subjects that are defined and certified by the parties in the contract itself and that must be identified, checked, read and interpreted by the smart contract on the basis of precise rules which in turn represent one of the most relevant parts and strategic aspects of the contract which obviously determine the final output.

**Smart contract as code execution**
Here comes the most relevant point relating to the substantial differences between traditional contract and smart contract. The smart contract is in fact a child of the execution of a code by a computer. It is a program that processes the information collected in a deterministic way (with identical results under identical conditions). In other words, if the inputs are the same, the results will be identical. This point is extremely relevant because, if on the one hand it represents a certainty and security as it guarantees the parties an absolute certainty of objective judgment excluding any form of interpretation, on the other it shifts the weight and responsibility or even the power to decide.

The contractors have the task of defining conditions, clauses, methods and rules of control and action, but once their contract has become a code and therefore a smart contract and the contractors accept it, the effects no longer depend on their will.

## Smart contract: insurance companies reward the adoption of the IoT on cars

An example comes from the world of motor vehicle insurance which on the basis of data collected thanks to Internet of Things equipment on board the cars are able to provide data on driver behavior that can influence and create certain conditions that activate or deactivate advantage clauses or downside. For example, exceeding speed limits determined by the contract can be read as conditions of greatest danger and lead to a contractual change in the conditions applied, for example in the value of the insurance premium.

Another example comes from the world of media where the provision and access to certain multimedia services is managed with digital rights management.

## The role of the lawyer and the developer

If the smart contract is called to do its job well, it must provide a series of guarantees to all parties involved and primarily at this point in our analysis the smart contract must ensure that the code with which it was written cannot be modified, that the data sources that determine the conditions of application are certified and reliable, that the methods of reading and checking these sources are in turn certified. The smart contract must be precise both in its drafting and in the management of the rules that determine its application and the rules that must govern any anomalies.

## Semantics and smart contract

We have seen that the concept and function of an automatic contract comes from afar, i.e., since Nick Szabo began working on the principle of automation of contractual functions. Smart contracts as we know them today need the blockchain to guarantee that trust in the relations between the various parties that no longer comes from a centralized third party, but from the community of the participants in the knowledge network itself, or development models that allow these tools to automate the relationships between the different parts to increase the ability to know the meanings and to constantly reduce the risk of error or misinterpretation.

Here, in this sense, one of the most important horizons comes from the union of research between the world of blockchain and that of semantics which helps systems to bring the understanding of meanings ever closer together. Thanks to the solutions for meta-learning applied to the smart contract sector, artificial intelligence, machine learning and blockchain are approaching.

## From smart contract to semantic contract

In this way the concept of automatic contract passes from the level of intelligent automatism to the form of semantic contract, that is, it takes the form of programmed automatism to learn and to modify one's behavior according to the acquired notions.

Thanks to this solution, smart contracts can reduce the possibility of errors and at the same time increase the knowledge of the contents by the systems and with this change the way in which the contracts are prepared and written to arrive at new automated forms of writing based on precisely on the principles of semantic learning.

## CHAPTER 7

# BITCOIN

In the cryptocurrency economy, miners (the users who make the computational resources available to the network to process the blocks) are rewarded in Bitcoin. And this, along with other elements, is one of the reasons why the system, as it was conceived eight years ago, begins to falter. After a couple of years of a roller coaster on the exchange value (which has fluctuated from 200 to over a thousand dollars per unit), experiments on university campuses, attempts to enter the stock market and dozens of scandals that have attracted media attention, Mike Hearn, developer of the technology and one of the most ardent supporters of Bitcoin, has publicly decreed the failure of the project. «It had to be a new form of decentralized currency, devoid of system institutions and too big to fail. But it has become something even worse: a mechanism completely controlled by a few people» wrote Hearn in a post announcing that he had sold all his Bitcoins. «In just eight months, the community, from being open and transparent, has become a place dominated by rampant censorship, with bitcoiners attacking other bitcoiners. Bitcoin has no future as it is controlled by less than ten people».

# What Are Bitcoins and How They Work

As already mentioned, the application, to date, most used for the blockchain (and which has made the blockchain famous in the world) is the Bitcoin system. Bitcoin can be considered a new currency, indeed as a cryptocurrency is defined.
Let's see in detail, and in a simplified way, how Bitcoins work.
To start using the Bitcoin currency as a trading currency, simply install an application for the Bitcoin wallet on your device (mobile, desktop, hardware or web). In practice, once the Bitcoin wallet has been installed, a first Bitcoin address will be generated, which can be shared with anyone, to allow them to send money to that address, then to the user who installed the Bitcoin wallet and shared your Bitcoin address. In theory, this address should only be used once, but it can also be used multiple times.
The whole Bitcoin system, as seen, is based on blockchain technology. In practice, all confirmed transactions are saved in the blockchain, and through your wallet you can check how many other Bitcoins you have available to make transactions. The whole system is protected by encryption, so as to be safe against cyber-attacks.

**The private key**
The money is transferred between two Bitcoin wallets, and the transaction is protected by a private key, that is a signature through which the transactions are signed, and which therefore allows you to guarantee that the money transferred is actually of the person who carried out the transaction and that no one changes this transaction, making the transaction secure. For more information on how Bitcoin works there are

some official documents such as the developer documentation and the Bitcoin wiki.

Bitcoins, despite being virtual, do not show substantial differences compared to traditional coins. In fact, they do not represent anything in the physical world, but they have value for the simple fact that people agree to exchange them for goods/services, in order to have an increasing number of them on their behalf, convinced that other people do the same.

The real revolution of Bitcoin lies in having built a control system - called blockchain - which, according to many, will be able to generate new disruptive paradigms for the financial and non-financial world.

## How bitcoin works

Unlike traditional currencies, Bitcoin does not use a central body, but relies on a distributed database, where all the nodes of the network that want to contribute to the system keep track of the individual transactions that have taken place.

Bitcoins, basically, are just files, which each user of the network can save in their own digital wallet (residing on their PC or on systems that emulate the service of traditional banks). Each Bitcoin address present in the wallet can be associated with a variable number of Bitcoins. Generally, to facilitate anonymity and make transactions less complicated, each of these is managed by generating a new address in which to receive the currency. Each address (public key) is associated with the equivalent of a digital signature (private key), which is useful for ensuring that only the owner of a certain address can initiate a transaction and it is linked.

Let's try to simplify how Bitcoin works. If we look at the Bitcoin protocol, a transaction can be read as a user's declaration to reduce his share of Bitcoin and to increase that of a second user by an equal value. When a transaction is managed, each node of the network participating in the system updates the register, transferring the information to the next node.

From a strictly operational point of view, the user (X) prepares an address (in the form of a public key), in which to receive the new transaction, while the second user (Y) identifies one of his addresses (which indicates a quantity Bitcoin specific) and starts the transaction. The transaction sees the second user (Y) add the public key prepared by the first (X) to his address, which will be joined to the private key in the digital signature role prepared to verify all the conditions of the transaction.

**How transactions are tracked**

In no node of the network is the balance of the accounts of individual persons kept track. Ownership of a certain share of Bitcoin is demonstrated by all previous transactions related to individual coins. Each transaction is in fact composed of a series of inputs (each refers to a Bitcoin address) that are precisely related to past transactions.

To transfer 10 bitcoins from one user (X) to another (Y), proceed in the following way. An input indicating a greater number of Bitcoins. In this case, two different transactions will be ordered from the network: the first that moves from user X to user Y all the amount linked to the input (e.g., 20 Bitcoins), the second that, essentially, balances with a calculation of the "change" the value to the user (e.g. 10 Bitcoin from Y to X). Two or more inputs (for example, two inputs respectively from 6 and 4 Bitcoins), which together (sum) perfectly represent the total of the transaction.

In particular, then the nodes of the network that verify a transaction exercise a control of the associated inputs, with the aim of validating the ownership of the sums. The check verifies up to the first Bitcoin transaction that has taken place. To make this operation possible, during the installation of a Bitcoin wallet, the overall history of all the operations carried out is downloaded, which are immediately processed to verify their authenticity, and which give rise to an operation that can take several hours to check. business suit.

## The security of Bitcoin

Bitcoin guarantees security to its users by exploiting control through the private key, which allows you to make sure that only the real owner of a certain amount of Bitcoin can create a transaction linked to that Bitcoin.

Security is also guaranteed by exploiting the control linked to the previous inputs, which are in turn used to ascertain that the sender really has the number of Bitcoins necessary to support the transaction.

## The risk of security vulnerabilities

Despite the measures described, there is the risk of a possible security vulnerability, linked to the order of transactions.

By launching two transactions - if they were to be potentially in conflict with each other, because they are linked to the same input - these could be randomly transferred across the network. In this circumstance, a node, which had already received the second transaction created, would also receive the first, with an unresolvable risk of ambiguity.

## The sidechain or second level chain

The issue of blockchain security and management of the governance of transactions on the blockchain has been at the center of attention for some time. Permissionless blockchains have a series of advantages that are consolidating over time while permissioned blockchains respond efficiently to a series of requirements but with a series of waivers compared to the blockchain paradigm. The search for a compromise between the two visions led to the experimentation and development of the sidechain or second level chain model. This is a solution that allows you to implement a sort of second level of exchange off the chain, that is, outside the main blockchain.

Thanks to the sidechains, a mechanism is activated that allows you to manage transactions or the exchange of tokens or other digital assets outside the blockchain that generated them, for example in another and different blockchain (private blockchain). Assets and tokens that can then be carried over to the original blockchain when needed. Sidechains can thus recover certain forms of security and governance that are not practicable in the world of public blockchains in other support or secondary (second level) blockchains. Specifically, sidechains can allow the management of exchanges between subjects active on the blockchain with management and registration on external environments (private blockchain) to the primary blockchain. In this way, the advantages of permissionless blockchains can be exploited in an integrated form with the control of permissioned blockchains used only for some specific needs. From a logical point of view, the sidechains are connected to the main blockchain in order to guarantee the interchangeability of the assets with a compromise between the opening and accessibility of the main blockchains (or main chain) and the efficiency and access control of the secondary blockchain.

# The Relationship Between Blockchain and Bitcoin

The term blockchain refers to the technological paradigm that allows the development of cryptocurrency-like applications: Bitcoin protocol represents only one - the first - of the possible achievements.

The association with the concept of Bitcoin may still generate some misunderstanding among the layman, but the blockchain - the technology underlying the mechanisms that regulate cryptocurrency transactions (of which the best known is Bitcoin) - seems destined to have a completely different role in the next stages of the development of world finance, and not only.

If even the Economist defined it in a cover story as the trust machine, giving it the power to transform the very functioning of the economy, it means that the P2P protocol developed in 2008 by Satoshi Nakamoto and adopted in years of a community made up of hackers, activists or, at best, speculators, has reached a level of maturity to convince even the most conservative analysts.

In particular, Bitcoin as a digital currency uses peer-to-peer technology and activates transactions that do not require central authorities or institutions. The issue of Bitcoin is carried out by the network and the management of transactions itself is governed by the Network. It is a collective operation in which all those who wish can participate by joining the project. Bitcoin technology is based on an open-source software and the development is public and shared. In other words, and in compliance with the vision indicated by Satoshi Nakamoto in his white book, the Bitcoin network is not owned or controlled by anyone, that is, it is owned and controlled by all those who intend to join the project.

# Not Just Bitcoin: the Application Areas of the Blockchain

The blockchain is not just Bitcoin. Virtual currency is in fact only one of its possible applications. Without centralized management, in fact, the blockchain allows you to send any data securely, drastically cutting the chain of intermediaries, and thus allowing a secure data exchange between two people and that's it, without having to use third-party means such as an e-mail provider, or an external Cloud Computing service.

## The important role of Finance and the growth of "non finance"

Much has been said about blockchain also at the World Economic Forum and there are many investors who are aiming for other investments in the blockchain sector, and therefore from the initial investments that there were only in the new currency and in new systems of payment, we finally move on to new investments, in new and different sectors.

## PWC

In an analysis carried out by PWC in 2018 with the involvement of 600 executives from 15 different countries, represented by 46 respondents, it emerged that 84 percent of respondents are involved. In particular, 20% are still engaged in research, 32% in the development phase, 10% work on pilot projects, 15% are with the blockchain in production while 7% say they have projects started, but for some reason then stuck. Only 14% have no involvement, active or expected on the blockchain.

**Deloitte**
According to Deloitte, more than 1 billion dollars have been invested in the blockchain, in over 120 startups connected to the blockchain, of which more than half of this money was invested only in 2016, an important confirmation came in 2017 and from the commitment and from the investments of many companies over the 2020-time horizon.

**Major new application areas of Blockchain in the world**

1) Blockchain in finance and banking
Finance and economics are certainly among the sectors most targeted by investors in relation to the blockchain. In fact, since there are no intermediaries to manage transactions, the blockchain would reduce the costs of banks' commissions, allowing savings, speed and reliability of transactions.
It therefore becomes essential to invest in this new technology for banks and financial institutions, which seek to grab a fairly large slice of this new market, which immediately reveals countless possibilities and opportunities.

2) Blockchain in insurance
Furthermore, as evidenced by a study conducted by Ernst Young, there is an excellent possibility of use for the blockchain in the insurance sector. Some ways blockchain can help insurance are accessing to secure and decentralized transactions, which provides a solid basis to prevent fraud, to ensure greater governance, to have better data and reporting. Furthermore, thanks to the blockchain, insurance companies can have up-to-date and accurate notifications in relation to

changes, and this allows them to improve risk management and maximize capital and fund opportunities, as well as the possibility of adopting big data strategies, which are very useful for obtaining secure information about their customers, their priorities and preferences, as well as any additional information taken from third parties.

From a technical point of view, insurers see blockchain as an opportunity to integrate a third-party ecosystem to reduce the costs of their management platforms, while improving customer experience and market share. and developing new solutions and opportunities.

Furthermore, at the market level, insurers have opportunities in the governance of their companies, through improved access to data, third-party controls, and more sophisticated risk management systems, associated with their products and services, such as cyber insurance.

## 3) Blockchain in digital payments

With regard to digital payments there are great opportunities for the blockchain. Obviously, there are still many problems that need to be addressed, such as the processing time of a transaction, which is still very slow considering the needs of a market and a world that go faster and faster. The performance of the system should also be improved, in order to be better absorbed by digital payments, and in the same way clear regulatory indications and a more careful analysis of threats and opportunities are the challenges of blockchain in the digital payments sector. Despite these challenges, however, there are many opportunities for this new technology applied to digital payments, and we will probably have the first feedback from the market very soon.

4) Blockchain in the agri-food sector
In the agri-food sector, the blockchain finds another excellent ally. Some of the application features of the blockchain in the agri-food sector are traceability, transparency, of those who want to tell the story of their food, using the blockchain to ensure reliability. Other companies already today want to track containers and transport of food and food in general using the blockchain. In conclusion, the benefits of the blockchain in agri-food sector are many, and from decentralization, to shared control, to immutability and preservation of information, there are certainly many applications for the blockchain in the agri-food sector.
In particular, the benefits of the blockchain appear particularly important for the processing industry and for all activities and developments related to food certification. The blockchain allows you to create open supply chains in which all the players: producers of raw materials, companies that deal with logistics and transport, companies that operate on raw materials at various levels of transformation, companies that work on packaging and marketing. finally, retail can provide data and information and control, with the utmost transparency, the data of all the other players. And the data related to each product can be put to the benefit of the final consumer. The blockchain in this way allows to create more open, more efficient and safer supply chains.

5) Blockchain in industry 4.0
Even in manufacturing, the blockchain can be a valid ally. Thanks to the blockchain in industry 4.0, in fact, it is possible to exploit the decentralized logic of the blockchain to produce technologies that can better support production, logistics and supply chain, as well as other core areas of the company.

Furthermore, thanks to the blockchain, it is possible to preserve the data and the security of the data itself, thus guaranteeing safety and reliability to the entire process of the production and distribution chain. The blockchain makes it possible to have solutions in particular for the processing industries, for the management of internal and external product logistics and for the management of supply chain relationships. In particular, solutions have been developed that make it possible to bring the logic of the trust which is widely used in the context of digital payments also in the context of transactions involving packets of data that represent the identity of certain products and their production logics. In these cases, it is necessary to have maximum reliability in terms of identity management and reliability. In this case, the blockchain can represent an excellent solution to implement the logic of industry 4.0 at the district and supply chain level.

6) Blockchain in the IoT

Blockchain is also very useful on the Internet of Things: thanks to its ease of data exchange, in fact, blockchain technology could be used to facilitate communication between connected IoT objects, as well as making the exchange of data safer and faster. The blockchain is then used as a platform for solutions that aim to manage the identity of things. Thanks to the correct identification of this identity, it is possible to create supply chain certification solutions based also on data coming from things (IoT) and work on supply chain certification. One of the most significant examples is that of the food supply chain.

But why is the - secure - recognition of objects so important and therefore the themes of identity management on the Internet of things? Today it is important to make the end-to-end recognition of virtual or physical objects more and more secure, because it is with these objects that the intermediation of people themselves in transactions takes place. That is, they are the objects that ultimately manage transactions. Today, thanks to user IDs and passwords or the use of special certificates, we are able to identify people, but people are identified thanks to objects. In certain cases - more and more frequent - there are objects that need to be identified without people behind them. So, if, thanks to the blockchain, objects can be identified, we would have a new identification tool, more secure, even for people.

Another crucial aspect is the role of IOTA to create inter-object payment solutions. The adoption of the blockchain in the world of the Internet of Things has made it possible to open new paths and new forms of service delivery in which customers are represented by "things". It became necessary to have solutions that would allow the development of forms of payment managed by the IoT and for the IoT. IOTA, was essentially created to create transaction systems in the IoT world and to make sure that transitions can take place without being subject to any type of commission. How this cryptocurrency works is completely different to other cryptocurrencies. At the base of everything is a special ledger, the tangle, a technology capable of operating using a decentralized register allowing IOTA to operate autonomously without the intervention of miners. Tangle represents a type of software protocol whose characteristics are well distinguished from those of the blockchain. The transactions, in fact, take place in parallel and have completely different peculiarities.

Also important in this area of payment is the role of a new phenomenon such as the In-Things Purchase which, thanks to the integration between smart connected products, identity management and payment systems, we could soon see the birth of new lines of business, in the form of "feature as a service". One of the levers for managing the In-Things Purchase is given, in perspective, precisely by tokenization.

7) Blockchain in healthcare

As regards blockchain and healthcare, managing patient medical data through a shared system would allow doctors to share information on patients in a safe and fast way, and therefore would greatly help medicine and healthcare to improve the service provided to patients, with the possibility of having the entire medical record of a patient under control, and therefore of knowing the patient's history in advance, in order to administer better and faster treatments.

The blockchain allows to give life to an organization that realizes the true centrality of the patient together with the intelligent coordination of all the medical actions that interest him. Considering that health services are provided by different structures with very different digital background, the blockchain can help give life to an intelligent coordination of all actions thanks to a review of management, interoperability between heterogeneous structures and information. Blockchain technologies, by their nature, can contribute to giving new answers in terms of progressive interoperability between national health information systems. The blockchain is also a response in terms of regulatory compliance (GDPR, Nis Directive) in complex scenarios that must manage the presence and interaction between interregional health systems, between private subjects such as analytical laboratories, private health structures or even insurance.

The blockchain opens up new scenarios to improve auditing procedures, for security, to reduce possible attacks, for the management of patient data to develop new authentication methods. Last but not least, the issue of smart contracts, which can speed up the control procedures and operating mechanisms of hospital structures and can, together with data management services, bring very important efficiencies in terms of secure document management. It should not be forgotten that in the healthcare world there is the great theme of the multitude of sources. For example, there is no single national register as regards pharmacological therapeutic prescriptions, but several sources, often fragmented together, must be coordinated, secure, decentralized and immutable document management can give new answers in terms of speed of access to the data needed when they are needed.

8) Blockchain in the public administration
The blockchain in the public administration also finds areas of application. The blockchain could in fact, for example, help the public administration and citizens to have a true digital identity, shared and implemented in this system, with several advantages including: making tax evasion more difficult, having greater control of citizens and therefore fighting the crime, simplified services in all sectors of the public administration (simplified data transmission), and much more.

9) Blockchain for e-voting or electronic voting
Electronic voting has long been the subject of experimentation, but the issue of security has always remained unsolved. There are numerous threats and risks associated with electronic voting and can be codified in 4 points:
1. manipulation of public opinion with actions aimed at influencing trends;
2. violation of identities;

3.  system intrusions and data manipulation;
4.  sabotage actions on voting shares.

10) Blockchain for risk management and governance in e-voting

As the experiences of different countries have shown, the answer can come from the blockchain. The unique digital assets or the possibility of guaranteeing the impossibility of duplication of a digital document and of fixing its uniqueness in a transparent and unchangeable way and the possibility of associating them securely with an identity represent one of the bases that allow the blockchain to bring new forms of guarantee in electronic voting.

In normal consultations, governance establishes risk management actions to reduce risks, while electronic voting requires specific governance, which indicates the correct behavior to reduce threats and to develop actions aimed at reducing risk factors.

Research firm CB Insight analyzed security needs in the world of electronic voting and to understand the role that the blockchain can play.

What can blockchain do for security in elections? There are several points on which the blockchain can bring a new approach and new solutions.

Before lessons, the blockchain can reduce the risks of incorrect media influence with solutions that direct control through cryptographic tools of media action and with mobile apps for voting management.

The blockchain can bring guarantees in the voting phase by managing the identity of the participants and verifying the uniqueness of the voting document.

After the vote, the blockchain allows audits to be carried out, guaranteeing transparency and immutability from possible violations.

## 11) Blockchain in retail

The blockchain seems to be an interesting model to be used in stores and in the retail field: with the blockchain, in fact, the current payment methods in the store could be extended to Bitcoin, thus allowing customers to pay much faster, as well as cheaper. By guaranteeing faster and cheaper payments, and therefore more convenient, a better service can be offered to the customer, which could therefore give a competitive advantage to the stores that will be the first to decide to enable these new technologies in their stores.

## 12) Blockchain in music

Copyright management has always been one of the most controversial and complex issues in the record market. This is a market that before and more than others has experienced a real transformation dictated by digital. Indeed, it can be said that this is a market that has experienced far more than one transformation and where the issue of remuneration of all the players in the supply chain has always been complicated to say the least. The exchange of musical pieces or their diffusion on a large scale, in the absence of a correct remuneration for the authors and for those who, as arrangers and musicians, contributed to the realization of the musical product, has caused discussion, and has seen attempts of all kinds. Thanks to the blockchain, smart contracts and the initiative of various startups, it is now possible to automate the remuneration, in part, of the supply chain of songwriters and collaborators, for every purchase choice we make.

The decisive point remains contained in the latter word: purchase choice. It must be a transaction, or the purchase of a song or the subscription to a service.

13) Blockchain and smart energy (smart grid)

The smart grid is a concept applied into the field of electricity. We have always been used to using electricity as consumers. We are certainly not used to living this dimension as producers, even if more and more often we find ourselves or we can find ourselves to be so.

The electricity grid is not a unique relationship from the producer to the customer but has a multiplicity of possibilities starting from the citizen who produces and makes his own energy available on the grid. But energy must be produced when needed or used when it is available in excess. In other words, we need an intelligent management of production and consumption. Smart grids use an analytics and exchange platform to manage consumption and production as precisely as possible and of course to minimize waste. The blockchain can play a very important role in the management of incoming and outgoing transactions in a way that allows the electricity grid to be made more democratic, or a way that also allows for the management of exchanges between those who have excess energy and those who have urgent needs. The research company Markets and Markets had forecast a 78% growth in 2018 in the use of blockchain for the energy market, but above all it foresees a development of the sector that should lead the blockchain - energy relationship to generate a business volume of over 7 billion of dollars in 2023 compared to a volume that was just under 400 million dollars in 2017. Payment management, Smart Contracts and pricing management are among the most important items that will support this demand.

But the blockchain is opening up many new perspectives to the world of energy, one of the most stimulating and important is that of P2P Energy, or the introduction of peer-to-peer exchanges in the energy market. By Peer-to-peer perspective we mean the world of end consumers who have chosen to produce energy for internal and personal or family use and who can be defined as prosumers (producers-consumers). Faced with a growth in the number of prosumers, micro-producers of energy, and thanks to the availability of tools and devices to make production more effective and consumption more efficient, there is the possibility of predicting an increase in the energy produced by these subjects, energy which can be brought to the market and which is now placed on the Internet.

But family or small business prosumers who aim for self-sufficiency and who find themselves having an energy surplus can legitimately aim to take advantage of it in a more direct way at the same time, large producers and distributors can think of a different system of relationships when the prosumers are organized and coordinated in an ecosystem of actors. Greater intelligence on production and consumption and a greater capacity for action by everyone to act on all levers can make it possible, for example, to reduce general consumption, make production more efficient and manage networks in a more stable and balanced way. In fact, they can make the energy machine that powers businesses and cities more efficient and less expensive. In all this, the energy peer-to-peer allows you to implement an energy transaction between peers, an exchange or sale of the energy surplus to other subjects with the same characteristics, for example between neighbors to whom to make their own energy available in excess and with the blockchain, there are the technological conditions to be able to manage a decentralized production and distribution organization.

The world of innovation and standardization looks carefully at this phenomenon and for example the Energy Web Foundation or EWF has launched a platform, the Energy Web Platform for the implementation and management of blockchain projects dedicated to the world of energy and is committed in the mapping and communication and dissemination of successful use cases in which the blockchain demonstrates its advantages for the sector and aims to promote its knowledge and replicability.

## 14) Blockchain and Central Banks: the CBDC, central bank digital currency

It goes without saying that banks have for some time been able to transform the threat that came from the blockchain into a great opportunity. An emblematic example comes from the Central Banks and therefore from the main institutions of the banking world which, as clearly highlighted by the report of the World Economic Forum WEF entitled "Central Banks and Distributed Ledger Technology: How Are Central Banks Exploring Blockchain Today?" They are actively working on projects that can take advantage of the blockchain. The report indicates 10 major priorities but the real key point, the one on which it is important to focus attention is the creation and support of a central bank digital currency, or CBDC.

It is a digital currency in the form of Digital Fiat Currency structured as the digital version of a currency exchange linked with the support of the Central Banks. However, the CBDC would have different characteristics from cryptocurrencies, which as it is well known are not issued by any state and have no legal coverage or value. CBDCs are not even in competition with the current banking system but represent an innovative monetary instrument in digital format valid as a payment instrument, as a store of value and as tools designed to increase security from the point of view of identification, traceability, prevention and reduction of counterfeiting and fraud risks.

Alongside CBDC, central banks have, according to the WEF report, the following 10 top priorities for blockchain:

1. retail central bank digital currency;
2. wholesale central bank digital currency;
3. interbank securities settlement;
4. payment system resiliency and contingency;
5. bond issuance and lifecycle management;
6. know-your-customer and anti-money-laundering;
7. information exchange and data sharing;
8. trade finance;
9. cash money supply chain;
10. customer SEPA Creditor Identifier (SCI) provisioning.

15) The blockchain for the unbanked

It is a bit bad to say, or rather to write, but it is a reality and a great opportunity both on a social and business level: to give a bank to those who do not have a bank, or to those who do not have access to banking and financial services. We are talking about the unbanked, 31% of the world population which in absolute terms means 1.7 billion people. For credit institutions looking for new business it would seem an "Eldorado" if this time the unbanked are not thinking about the banks but a name that we all know well and that under normal conditions we would struggle to associate with the job of the bank. We are talking about Facebook, which is among the promoters of the Libra project, the association (The Libra Association) that is preparing to give life to a cryptocurrency,

Libra, which also has the mission of serving all those who are unable to have a bank today and who tomorrow will be able to pay, send and receive money, and manage financial services thanks to their smartphones.

The Libra Association is not, as Valeria Portale, Director of the Blockchain & Distributed Ledger Observatory of the Polytechnic University of Milan observes, an attack on banks, but it can certainly bring to the real world a new way of managing payments and services that can help change the competitive banking landscape. Thus, the relationship between the blockchain and credit institutions continues to be controversial, in a sort of love and hate, as we see in the following chapter.

## From an alternative to traditional finance to an ally of the banks

After all, the interest of the banks has no longer been a secret for some time. Goldman Sachs said blockchain is set to revolutionize the industry, while Barclays and USB have publicly admitted that they could use the technology in a variety of operational areas, from remittances to contracts. Bank of England said it has created a number of development teams within its organization. Instead, in September, R3 was born, a private consortium of financial institutions interested in the potential of the Blockchain. In December there was a new round of subscriptions, which saw the entry of BMO Financial Group, Danske Bank, Intesa Sanpaolo, Natixis, Nomura, Northern Trust, OP Financial Group, Banco Santander, Scotiabank, Sumitomo Mitsui Banking Corporation, US Bancorp and Westpac Banking Corporation. Today 42 institutes have joined the federation in all.

But there are also those who have already gone from words to deeds: Bank of America has filed with the U.S. Patents and

Trademark Office (USPTO) 15 blockchain-related patents and is expected to file another twenty in these days. According to what has been made public by the USPTO, Bank of America's patents aim to create systems for identifying risks related to cryptocurrencies and alerting suspicious users.

Obviously, there is no lack of the downside. If on the one hand banks are attracted by the possibility of activating cheaper and safer transactions, on the other the idea that those who participate in the network can see in real time the data circulating through the nodes considerably cools the enthusiasm of those who do not want that their transactional flows become public. It is therefore necessary to ensure that each user has the credentials to see only the operations that concern him. This is one of the most debated topics at the blockchain conference in London: together with those of the regulation and complexity of the data protection tools to be adopted at the level of international jurisdiction, it has been indicated as one of the most delicate issues for the diffusion of technology.

## The other possible application areas, from PA to businesses

It's not just banks that consider blockchain a strategic development lever. If many observers say they are convinced that even the practices of the public administration and even personal data and identity documents can be managed by exploiting the distributed control systems offered by the blockchain (even applicable to notarial activities or the management of intellectual property), let's start to evaluate the positive impact of technology on private companies as well.

Also, in London, the usefulness of the blockchain to simplify business processes, reducing costs and increasing the efficiency of finance departments was discussed. An initial inclusion in internal flows is envisaged, creating user groups with specific access levels, keeping all operations transparent and facilitating analytical activities thanks to the speed and homogeneity of the data transmitted.

The next step? The implementation in business networks, with the automation of procurement processes through real-time notification systems, the constant and shared monitoring of the assets available for sale and purchase and, again, the generation of precise, gradual barriers to entrance for participation in the exchange. It would be a quantum leap, but the adaptability shown by businesses strengthened by digital disruption bodes well.

Much, however, can also depend on the will of technology vendors to first understand, then embrace and finally implement the logic of the blockchain in their offer. There are those who are already thinking about it. But the game is interdisciplinary, as well as international, and in addition to developing technical solutions that respond to concrete - and still unsolved - problems, an important work of information and awareness is also needed to involve institutions and associations in the definition of adequate regulatory systems.

**Blockchain, standards and institutions**
Companies, organizations and above all public administrations, when they have to face analysis and decision processes regarding the evaluation and adoption of innovative technologies such as blockchain, direct their research on three major information areas:

- the possibility of accessing documented case histories that can provide guidance on the results of concrete experiences;
- the availability of shared standards or, where these are not yet available, the visibility with respect to working groups, international discussion tables working on these issues;
- the knowledge of the professionals, skills or paths and actors in terms of training who are in a position to make available figures with appropriate skills.

## CHAPTER 8

# ETHEREUM

Ethereum is a computational platform that is paid through exchanges based on a cryptocurrency calculated in Ether. It is a platform that can be adopted by all those who wish to become part of the network, and who in this way will have at their disposal a solution that allows all participants to have an immutable and shared archive of all the operations implemented during the time and which at the same time is conceived in order not to be stopped, blocked or censored. Ethereum could be presented as the largest shared computer that is capable of delivering enormous power available everywhere and forever. So, with Ethereum we move from the concept of distributed database to distributed computing. Ethereum is designed to be adaptable and flexible and to easily create new applications. Ethereum is a programmable blockchain that does not limit itself to making predefined and standardized operations available but allows users to create their own operations. In fact, it is a blockchain platform that allows you to create various types of decentralized blockchain applications not necessarily limited to cryptocurrencies only.

## Ether: Ethereum's Trading Currency

The use of Ethereum's computational resources is remunerated with a special virtual currency called Ether, which itself represents both the processing power needed to produce the contracts and the cryptocurrency that allows you to pay for the execution of the contracts. Ether is basically and concretely a token that is treated as a cryptocurrency exchange with the ETC ticker symbol.

Ethereum then relies on an internal transaction pricing mechanism called "Gas", which has the purpose of optimizing network resources, preventing spam and allocating resources in a proportionate and correct manner according to requests.

**Ethereum Virtual Machine EVM: the engine of Ethereum**
Ethereum is a "Turing complete" system that allows developers to create applications that run on the EVM using programming languages that in turn refer to traditional platforms such as JavaScript and Python.

The Ethereum engine is represented by the Ethereum Virtual Machine (EVM), which actually represents the runtime environment for the development and management of smart accept Ethereum. EVM operates in a protected manner, namely, it is completely separate from the network. The code managed by the virtual machine does not have access to the network and the smart contracts generated are independent and separate from other smart contracts.

In 2016 Ethereum was split into two different blockchains Ethereum Classic and Ethereum Foundation.

# Ethereum Foundation

Ethereum Foundation is the organization that aims to manage all development, research and support activities of the Ethereum platform. In 2014 when the developer team composed of Vitalik Buterin together with Anthony Di Iorio, Mihai Alisie and Charles Hoskinson Ethereum also became a reality in the form of a business with the Swiss company Ethereum Switzerland GmbH. It was then the non-profit Ethereum Foundation that took the reins of the project.

Ethereum was characterized by a series of prototypes and development actions financed and managed by the Ethereum Foundation on the basis of the proof of concept and project up to the launch of the frontier network project in order to improve security and usability. Among the various initiatives, the Olympic project should be noted which, among other things, had the aim of testing the performance and limits of the Ethereum blockchain network with a stress test.

With the Olympic project comes the aforementioned frontier network. More recently, the Ethereum Foundation is involved in the Homestead project designed to improve the transactional component, the logic of Gas for pricing management and security. Alongside Homestead, the Metropolis project is active, aimed at simplifying the use of the Ethereum Virtual Machine and allowing developers to act with greater flexibility and speed. Yet another project, Serenity should bring a series of innovations in the management logic of the algorithm that manages Ethereum's consensus.


## Ethereum Classic


Ethereum classic is the result of an important division in the original core of Ethereum at the level of the Ethereum Foundation. In particular, Ethereum Classic is made up of Ethereum members who have decided to give life to a new version of Ethereum, in fact not sharing the development lines of the Ethereum Foundation. Ethereum Classic is managed by a different team than the Ethereum Foundation.

Ethereum Classic is a network that in the intentions of its promoters remains 100% compatible with Ethereum technology, but with a series of services designed to increase security and usability. Ethereum Classic is based on the development of a non-hackable blockchain and has developed a strategy of issuing tokens in proportion to the development of the network over time, in order to limit the risks of deflation of the cryptocurrency.

## What happened with the DAO and why it matters to Ethereum

The DAO event (acronym for Decentralized Autonomous Organization) gave rise to the fork of the Ethereum blockchain and is important for understanding the evolutionary logic and rules of the blockchain itself.

The DAO was in effect a decentralized autonomous organization, an organization created on the Ethereum blockchain characterized by the fact of being a virtual organization, that is, without a headquarters, without a legal personality, without clearly identifiable figures as administrators. The DAO intended to raise capital (through the exchange of DAO Tokens for ETH) to invest in projects that were previously evaluated by a committee and then put to the vote to the holders of the DAO Token. The latter could cast their vote (proportional to the quantity of DAO tokens possessed) to determine which projects the capital would then be disbursed to.

Specifically, the DAO was created with a series of steps typical of an ICO: website to provide information, dissemination of a whitepaper describing the project, audit of the source code of the smart contracts used, agreements with some exchanges for allow the exchange of tokens once acquired, etc.

Within a few months the organizers of the DAO managed to raise about 150 million dollars. But due to a violation of the address in which the ETH received by the organization were allocated on June 18, 2016, about 70 million dollars were lost in a few hours.

In the case of the DAO, the investors had exchanged Ether (which had a determined value on the market) for DAO tokens; the investment was made with an expectation of profit (which can generally be dividends, periodic payments, increase in value).

The DAO's promotional materials highlighted the goal of creating a for-profit entity, aimed at financing projects in exchange for a return on investment; the expectation of return on investment depended on the management efforts of others, since the organization of The DAO on the decisions regarding the projects to be financed was absolutely top-down.

These considerations led the SEC to consider DAO tokens financial instruments, with consequent application of the law from which derives the obligation for the issuing body to register the offers and sales of the instruments and, correlatively, with consequent registration obligation for the subjects which offered trading platforms for the aforementioned tokens such as national securities exchanges.

## Ethereum VS Ethereum Classic

Ethereum represents the official version of the blockchain and is managed and updated by the developers who designed and built it, while Ethereum Classic is a blockchain that, starting from Ethereum, stands as an evolution or as a form of alternative. The reason that led to this division is linked to a specific hacking event that hit an Ethereum project (precisely, the DAO) and that had induced the Ethereum community to change the Ethereum code to remedy the consequences of this hacker attack. This decision has opened a rift on the very concept of blockchain, or on the underlying principles of this paradigm. On the one hand there were all those who argued that blockchains live on the principle of the community and it is the majority of the community that decides on the possible evolutions of the blockchain itself. And based on this belief, if the majority of the community agrees, the blockchain can be modified. Then there is a different school of thought which instead argues that the blockchain cannot be modified, it must be firmly protected from any form of tampering. This division put the developers at a crossroads and the so-called purists, when Ethereum created a new blockchain, chose to continue operating on the old version of the blockchain. Specifically, with this step, two Ethereum blockchains were created, and in particular Ethereum Classic, operates today as a parallel version of the blockchain.

# Ethereum 2.0

What is Ethereum 2.0 and why does its arrival took on fundamental importance within the cryptocurrency sector? The long-awaited Ethereum update - which takes the name of Ethereum 2.0 - aims to solve network problems related to scalability and security. In its first phase, which started on 1 December 2020, the blockchain system switched to a proof of stake mechanism.

Summing up: Ethereum, the second strongest cryptocurrency in the world by market capitalization, will soon undergo an implementation of its network; the upgrade - called Ethereum 2.0 - aims to improve the security and scalability of the network. The first phase of the upgrade - which has been already inaugurated on 1 December - consisted in the transition of Ethereum towards a proof of stake mechanism.

## What is Ethereum 2.0?

Ethereum 2.0 aims to improve the scalability and security of the network through a series of changes to its infrastructure, in particular the transition from a consensus proof of work mechanism to a proof of stake mechanism.

As anticipated, Ethereum 2.0 - also known as Eth2 or "serenity" - is an upgrade to the Ethereum blockchain. This wants to make the speed, efficiency and scalability of the network more efficient so that the latter can process a greater number of transactions, while avoiding overload situations.

Ethereum 2.0 will be released in several phases: the first of these (Phase 0) has already started on December 1, 2020. However, the launch on that date is subject to the achievement of certain criteria: the presence of 16,384 validators, with the payment of 32 ETH each for a total required of 524,288 Ether within the new system.

## What changes with Ethereum 2.0

Ethereum 1.0 uses a consensus mechanism called proof of labor (PoW), while Ethereum 2.0 will use a proof of stake (PoS) mechanism.

But what's the difference between the two? With a blockchain like that of Ethereum, it is necessary to validate transactions in a decentralized way. Ethereum, like other cryptocurrencies, currently uses proof of work (PoW).

In this mechanism, miners use the processing power of computer hardware to solve complex mathematical puzzles and verify new transactions. The first miner to solve the puzzle adds a new transaction to the record of all transactions that make up the blockchain and is rewarded with cryptocurrencies in return. However, this process can take a lot of energy.

In the Proof of Stake (PoS) it is necessary to prove that you are in possession of cryptocurrencies in order to participate in the draw and have the right to verify a transaction. These entities can propose to create a block based on the amount of cryptocurrency held and for how long they have held it.

Other validators can then certify that they have seen this block. When there are enough claims, a block can be added to the blockchain. The validators are then rewarded for the successful block proposal. This process is known as "forging" or "minting".

The main advantage of PoS lies in the fact that it is much more energy efficient than PoW, since it no longer requires the energy expenditure necessary for the computer to process the algorithm. Strong computing power is therefore not required to secure the blockchain.

## Ethereum 2.0 improves scalability and security

As already explained, the main objective of the update is to make scalability and security more efficient. Let's see below how.

1) Scalability

How will Ethereum 2.0 make it more scalable than Ethereum 1.0? With Ethereum 1.0, the network can only support around 30 transactions per second, which causes delays and congestion situations. Ethereum 2.0 promises to bring the transition number per second to 100,000. This increase will be possible through the implementation of shard chains (secondary chains on the blockchain) - the second upgrade of Eth2. These will increase the network capacity and improve the speed of transactions by extending the network to 64 blockchains.

The current configuration of Ethereum provides for a blockchain consisting of a single chain with consecutive blocks. This makes it safe, but very slow and inefficient. With the introduction of shard chains, this blockchain is divided, allowing transactions to be managed in parallel rather than consecutive chains.

2) Security

Ethereum 2.0 was conceived with the security issue in mind. Most proof of stake networks have a small group of validators, which makes the system more centralized and reduces network security. Ethereum 2.0 instead requires the presence of a minimum of 16,384 validators, which makes everything much more decentralized and therefore secure.

But there are also vulnerabilities: the proof of stake participation rate. The Ethereum Foundation is creating a dedicated Ethereum 2.0 security team to research possible cybersecurity issues in cryptocurrency.

**The different phases of Eth2**

After a series of test launches - Topaz, Medalla, Spadina and Zinken - the full roll-out of Ethereum 2.0 will take place in three phases: Phase 0, 1 and 2 (developers, you know, like to count from zero).

Phase 0 has already started on 1 December, while the others will take place over the next few years.

Phase 0

Phase 0 involves the implementation of the Beacon Chain; this stores and manages the register of validators as well as distributing the proof of stake (PoS) mechanism for Ethereum 2.0. The Ethereum PoW chain, the original one, has run alongside the other, so there are no interruptions in the continuity of the data.

Phase 1

Phase 1, expected in 2021, will see the integration of the proof of stake in the shard chains. The launch of 64 of the latter is expected, although at the time of their launch they will not support either accounts or smart contracts.

Step 1.5

Phase 1.5, a provisional update scheduled for 2021, will bring with it the official transfer to the proof of stake.

Phase 2

Phase 2, scheduled for 2021/2022, will see the shards become fully functional and compatible with smart contracts. Ether accounts will be integrated, transfers and withdrawals enabled, cross-shard transfers and contract calls implemented. It will create execution environments for scalable apps based on Ethereum 2.0.

**The effects on the Ethereum listing**

For many, the launch of Eth2 is just what Ethereum needed. «Once Ethereum scales through Eth 2.0 technology, all questions will be answered» told Jamie Anson, founder of Nifty Orchard and organizer of Ethereum London.

Greater scalability means greater utilization, which, in turn, leads to increased demand. Which, at least in theory, should push Ethereum's price to new levels.

## CHAPTER 9

# CRYPTOCURRENCY: WHO WILL BE THE NEXT BITCOIN

Even if Bitcoin and Ethereum continue to dominate the scene, there are several suitors who are candidates to become mainstream. Particularly focus on those cheaper tokens like Cardano and IOTA. Not just Bitcoin and Ethereum. The growing presence of crypto-assets in investors' portfolios is accentuating the phenomenon of diversification.

The market is evolving. Instead of staying focused only on Bitcoin and Ethereum, where investors can only hold a fraction of a coin, we are witnessing a growth in demand for coins that quote to a level like Bitcoin and Ethereum was a few years ago, noted Simon Peters, eToro's crypto expert.

Let's try to see, through the analysis of data relating to trading volumes on crypto-assets recorded in February on the eToro multi-asset investment platform, what the new Bitcoin could be. In the last month Cardano (ADA) has become the second most traded crypto-asset since the beginning of the year after Bitcoin on the eToro platform.

In the wake of indications regarding the development of the "Goguen" update, Cardano in the last week of February hit a new high of $1.4536 (on eToro, which is one of the few regulated platforms on which private clients can hold Cardano).

Another crypto-asset in turmoil in February was IOTA (MIOTA) which saw trade growth of 274%, referring to the Italian context, month over month (+ 265% globally), which projected it among the top five currencies in terms of volumes on eToro.

The drive to demand is linked to the statements of its co-founder, Dominik Schiener, who announced the forthcoming launch of the anticipated digital assets framework.

The "Chrysalis" update to the "Internet of Things" blockchain network will allow trading on the platform without delays, and in a faster and more efficient way.

The continuing trend of diversification in the world of crypto-assets has seen a surge in demand from Binance's private clients, with a four-digit increase in trading (+ 1066%) compared to a 1047% increase globally, always month on month.

Activity more than doubled on both Tron and Dash, respectively up 198% (+ 174% globally) and 132% (+ 125% globally) compared to January.

"Investors - continues Peters - are on the hunt for the new Bitcoin, in the sense that they are investing in cheaper tokens such as Cardano, IOTA and Tron, which all trade around one dollar. We think that in the current year the hunt for the new bitcoin will intensify as the market is expanding and other currencies are gaining support."

## Bitcoin is confirmed in the first position

Also in February, Bitcoin is confirmed as the most traded crypto on eToro and this despite a 24% drop in demand. A negative sign also for the demand for Ethereum, whose exchanges on eToro fell by 12%.

February was another busy month for Bitcoin and Ethereum. Both cryptocurrencies have seen their prices soar since the beginning of the year, but while there has been volatility, the fact that their acceptance is increasing continues to give strength to both crypto assets. With the growth of real cases of crypto use, it is no longer a question of 'if', but of when they will spread in everyday life. We expect volatility to persist because, as with all emerging assets, the crypto journey is only just beginning.

# CHAPTER 10

# ICO

## ICO Blockchain

One of the developments of the blockchain concerns the field of crowdfunding and financing in the form of venturing for startups. The ICO (Initial Coin Offering) is an innovative crowdfunding method totally based on cryptocurrencies.

The Initial Coin Offering (otherwise also defined as Initial token offering or as token sale) is bringing a series of important innovations to the world of venturing and represents in effect a sort of IPO (Initial Public Offering) entirely managed with cryptocurrency on the blockchain.

The ICO is a revolutionary tool in the world of venturing because it allows us to overcome the rigid rules of the evaluation processes traditionally followed by funds and banks to which we have been accustomed in recent years. However, this is an operation that is aimed at new companies operating in the field of blockchain or that have developed or are developing solutions based on the blockchain. In practice, the ICO is implemented with the sale of tokens by the startup that is looking for resources on the market. Tokens can be traded with cryptocurrencies such as Bitcoin or Ether. The investment proposal that is implemented precisely through the sale of tokens is based on the presentation of an industrial plan or business project. The ICO, like the IPO, is designed to give trust and resources to an idea, which specifically aims to grow the blockchain and finds its consensus in the community that operates on the blockchain. The tokens, object of the investment, can be effectively exchanged and, like the shares of a listed company, can see their nominal value vary according to many factors, starting from the performance of the project presented and the fluctuations of the cryptocurrencies.

# What Exactly Is an Initial Coin Offering?

The issue of tokens for the remuneration of verification and control services has allowed the creation of a new financing method that has taken the name of Initial Coin Offering precisely because of the role that Coins are called upon to play in favoring development of the company itself. The token is issued to investors in exchange for digital currency and at the same time investors can use the tokens received to enjoy the innovative services provided by the startup or they can sell them when the market appreciates them and can guarantee a markup. The American startup Protocol Labs Inc., for example, has received a loan of several million dollars thanks to an ICO in order to build a blockchain network where storage space can be purchased and sold using Filecoin or tokens issued by Protocol. same for the ICO funding request. In this way, if the company is successful in creating this digital storage marketplace, the value of Filecoins is likely to rise. The lenders can use the Filecoins to buy storage space, or they can exchange them to sell their stake in the company with the Filecoins themselves.

To understand the value of the ICO it is necessary to look at the logic of crowdfunding. If you think that in 2015 alone crowdfunding platforms made it possible to raise funding for something like 34 billion dollars, you understand the reasons for the consensus that surrounds and accompanies this method of financing for startups and investors. The ICO takes crowdfunding to a new level, thanks to the help of technology and thanks to the logic of the blockchain, it is possible to link the value of the investment with the value of the community that believes in that investment. Tokens express the value of the asset and are a security that can be used by all participants to actively contribute to running the company in which it is invested and to increase its value.

The technological aspect of tokens and therefore of ICOs is complex and articulated, but there is one point that should be emphasized in particular. The transactional conditions linked to the tokens are not only defined during the ICO phase but are written in the code of the tokens. The ICO can rely on the logic of smart contracts, ensuring maximum transparency and openness and traceability on every single transaction. Auditing operations, for example, can be speeded up and even automated. The transparency linked to automated smart contracts allows the creation of guarantee accounts for the management of funds linked to the recognition of values that are activated only when certain objectives are reached, automatically verified, and controlled by smart contracts.

# The Substantial Difference Between ICO and IPO

If on the one hand ICO and IPO respond to the same need with a similar implementation logic, it must be said that in the case of the IPO, all operations are subject to the control of a supervisory institution which in our country is represented by Consob which monitor the correctness of the purchasing procedures and the operations of the companies involved. In the case of the ICO, there is no reference body for control.

**From ICOs to STOs, towards greater security**
Initial Coin Offerings have raised many objections and not a few perplexities, they have often been used as a vehicle for financial speculation and in many cases the industrial project did not live up to expectations or was not there at all.
The STOs, Security Token Offering must be read as an evolution of the ICOs, Initial Coin Offering that concern not only the world of blockchain-based companies, but all companies that can have assets of tokenizable value. It is necessary to think that the ICOs had the purpose, in a nutshell, to allow companies to implement a sort of crowdfunding by selling tokens representing an asset. Specifically, then reality has shown that the ICOs that have been able to express a value for both parties were those built on a token able to represent a real service and able to monetize it, or to make sure that the token was in the condition to become an exchange asset for transactions aimed at buying or selling the service and not as an asset created as an exclusive form of investment.
STOs provide investors with greater security and greater control and are less prone to fraud. Security tokens precisely because they are the digital representation of a concrete real asset registered and managed on the blockchain offer a series of advantages over ICO utility tokens, such as financial rights. If the utility tokens that provide access to a service or an asset within a specific environment or ecosystem of operators, the security tokens instead represent the real asset and can be considered to all intents and purposes as a form of investment,

the benefits of which can be realized in various forms, from the traditional right to a dividend or expected interest, to the possibility of enjoying rights that represent the investment itself in the governance of the company. Precisely because they are in all respects forms of investment, security tokens are subject to regulation. In other words, security tokens are the representation, on the blockchain, of traditional financial instruments such as shares or bonds, they are instruments subject to existing financial regulation and provide for forms of control and security for investors.

# CHAPTER 11

# BLOCKCHAIN AND GDPR

The GDPR was created to regulate the management of privacy linked to the use of user data on the web, apps and social media by web and media companies that are trying to build their own competitive advantage on user profiling. It is very important to understand the relationship between blockchain and GDPR because it can open up new forms of security management in the form of privacy by design. The GDPR can be interpreted as a charter of digital rights of the people.

## GDPR Legislation in Summary

The heart of the GDPR is the protection of people's data, in other words of the individuals to whom such data belongs. In a very concise way, this is what the GDPR introduces on the subject:

- ❖ art. 12: people have the right to ask and have answers on the use that a company will make of their data and to ask for compensation if these questions do not have clear, concise and timely answers;

- ❖ articles 13 and 14: users have the right to know how personal data will be used at the time of their collection/request and to know how long they will be kept;
- ❖ art. 15: users have the right to know and access personal data that are processed by those who have requested their consent;
- ❖ art. 16: people can rectify and modify their personal data (+ art. 19: who collects the data must also inform the third parties allowed to use them to stop using the rectified or deleted data);
- ❖ art. 17: users have the right to request (and obtain) the cancellation of their personal data when they are no longer necessary for the purposes for which they were collected;
- ❖ art. 18: individuals can limit the processing of their data when they are inaccurate, when they have been collected illegally or not following legal procedures;
- ❖ art. 20: users have the right to their personal data in a structured and commonly used format so that they can be easily read by any machine (PC, smartphone, app, etc.);
- ❖ Art. 21: people have the right to object to the use of their data for profiling or marketing and must be enabled to say "no".

**The role of legislation and privacy**

According to the World Economic Forum, by 2025 as much as 10% of the world's GDP will be produced by activities and services that will be delivered and distributed through blockchain technologies. In this scenario, governance management in relation to regulations appears fundamental, first of all the GDPR, the general European regulation on data protection.

**The possible relationships between GDPR and blockchain**
The GDPR regulation impacts on a series of areas that pertain to the specific characteristics of the blockchain:
- data access and visibility: the data entered in the blockchains is public and accessible by anyone participating in the chain;
- data deletion: data stored in a blockchain is tamper-proof, so their deletion will not be possible once such data is entered into the distributed chain;
- data immutability over time: the data present in the blockchains are kept indefinitely and cannot be modified, tampered with or deleted;
- distributed data control: blockchains are distributed therefore control over data cannot be centralized and is in the hands of all participants in the blockchain (i.e. it is difficult to identify the Data Protection Officer figures required by the GDPR);
- automated decision-making processes - with smart contracts, automated decision-making processes must also be considered, i.e. a new type of data management.

**Blockchain and GDPR for Security by design**

Blockchain and GDPR makes it possible to create security by design solutions ensuring pseudonymization (decoupling of data from individual identity) and data minimization (sharing only the absolutely necessary data points).

We remind you that in the blockchain data protection is ensured by a public key of the sender of the transaction; from a public key of the recipient of the transaction; from a cryptographic hash of the transaction content; from the date and time of the transaction.

With this setting it is impossible to reconstruct the content of a transaction from the one-way cryptographic hash, and unless one of the parties to the transaction decides to link a public key to a known identity, it is not possible to map and link transactions to individuals or organizations. This means that even though the blockchain is public (where anyone can see all transactions on it), no personal information is made public.

# Blockchain, GDPR and Legislative Issues

The GDPR introduces some rules that may not always be respected by blockchains.

GDPR e Data Protection Officer

The GDPR introduces the figure of the DPO - Data Protection Officer, a person expert in legislation and practices relating to data protection who must assist the person who controls or manages them in order to verify internal compliance with the regulation. The DPO must be a person with a good command of IT processes, data security and other business consistency issues regarding the maintenance and processing of personal and sensitive data.

When is it necessary to appoint a personal data controller? In the GDPR, the controller must be appointed in the event that the main processing activities require regular and systematic monitoring of data subjects on a large scale, in the event that the activities involve the large-scale processing of particular categories of personal data or of data relating to criminal convictions and offenses, even when the processing is carried out by a public authority or a public body.

## Which jurisdiction to apply for which country's law

In case of disputes, which laws should apply and whose jurisdiction is it? In situations where it is not possible to identify the entity of processing of personal data and the place where the data is processed, it is difficult to identify the jurisdiction which should be responsible for any legal assessment of data processing.

## Identification of personal data

In a blockchain context what can be recognized as personal data? The identity of a user (and therefore his sensitive data) is protected by a code that represents the public key to join the distributed network. From a regulatory point of view, it is necessary to understand what constitutes personal data in a blockchain context: should public keys be considered personal data? Although a public key appears as pseudonymized data, these do not represent anonymous data and are very often associated with specific natural persons.

## Data disseminated on each node of the network

Does the blockchain limit the purpose of data collection and processing and their minimization? In a blockchain (especially if it is public) data is kept on every node of the network - publicly accessible to anyone - regardless of the original purpose for which that data was entered and processed in the blockchain. How does this typical feature of the blockchain fit into a regulatory context that provides that the specific purposes for which personal data are processed must be specified, explicit and legitimate and that personal data must be adequate, relevant and limited to the purposes for which are treated.

## Immutability

Blockchains are practically immutable and the data they contain is often impossible to update, delete, modify or correct. Therefore, it is also necessary to address at the regulatory level how can the issue of the right to be forgotten be managed within a blockchain?

## CHAPTER 12

# GOVERNANCE OF THE BLOCKCHAIN

In public blockchains, participation, in all its forms, is largely defined by the structure of the blockchain itself. In private blockchains, governance is absolutely crucial and directly affects the feasibility of projects, the chances of success and the achievement of objectives. In particular, the issue of governance can be divided into four areas:

- general governance: it is an area that relates to the ecosystem of the blockchain and defines the references, the criteria of responsibility and the decision-making processes of the blockchain itself, the roles, responsibilities, functions and decision-making criteria. The question of the ownership of the blockchain, or rather of the actors who promote and guide the development of the blockchain, also fits into ecosystem governance;

- technological governance: these are rules and decisions that put the blockchain in relation with the legacy IT world, with Big Data, with the Internet of Things, with artificial intelligence and with all the

technological contexts that are supported or relate to the blockchain;
- data governance: in this area, the governance relating to data management is addressed in terms of regulatory compliance, for example for security and privacy;
- governance of results: the last aspect (for the moment) is that of governance in the measurement and distribution of the benefits of the blockchain. The more projects that involve extensive and complex supply chains become consolidated, the more it will be necessary to define rules for the measurability of results and for the distribution of benefits.

**What does data time validation mean**

The certification and validation of a data consists of multiple factors, among these a particularly important role is played by the so-called time validation. In the case of eIDAS, for example, a rule has been established according to which the digital time validation relates to those data that connect other data in electronic form on a specific date (time, date) such that even from the point from a temporal point of view there is certain proof of their existence at that particular moment also in terms of relationship with other data. One of the themes that accompany the legal development of the blockchain is also that of the validation of legal effects and their use in legal forms. The time validation systems are therefore an enabler not only of the time factor but thanks to the time factor and an associated electronic seal or signature it allows to increase the level of safety relating to absolute reliability of that data. In other words, the security of the quality, integrity and reliability of the data on the blockchain also passes through the time verification tool.

# Corporate Governance and Blockchain

The innovations of the blockchain will change the way companies are managed and governed with a fundamental impact for management, investors and all other stakeholders. There are numerous companies that are studying how to use blockchains for the management of property registers in many private activities and in the world of public administrations, government applications allow the management of residence and birth certificates, real estate titles, university degrees. and much more with the blockchain. And if attention is drawn to the use of the blockchain for registering the ownership of company shares, it is possible to combine ledger management with smart contracts to create forms of automation, for example in the provision of options for employees or property titles for external investors. Blockchains are in a position to create a situation of greater transparency that allows investors to monitor ownership positions and reduce the risk of corruption. If a company chooses to publish and archive its financial documents on a public blockchain, the financial reporting and communication strategies would change dramatically in favor of greater transparency and a simultaneous reduction in costs.

# Distributed Blockchain and Database

Faced with an "Internet" model that replicates the "centralized" logic of "enterprise" models, or infrastructures that allow centralized management and control, a model that goes in the direction of de-centralization is spreading, thanks also to the blockchain and that for many it represents a model capable of bringing about greater "democratization", both in terms of accessibility and in terms of the possibility and opportunity of sharing information and decision-making processes.

The blockchain allows (or rather, can allow) to give life to a decentralized Internet, where essentially no single entity owns or controls the IT infrastructure.

## What is IPDB, the decentralized database based on blockchain

Here is an example of a decentralized database created by BigchainDB, based on blockchain technology, governed by a non-profit body and ready to use, allowing to combine the security of the blockchain with the searchability of database-style information.

IPDB is a database with a global vision and with a governance it is entrusted to a non-profit foundation. The members of the foundation are the custodians of the network and each of them manages a server node that stores and validates transactions. Together these nodes make up the IPDB database.

IPDB, can be identified as:

1) network that manages a decentralized database;

2) non-profit association, whose network forms membership in a transparent way (following the Trust principles typical of the blockchain).

IPDB is also based on the technologies already developed by BigchainDB, that is a Big Data database also designed for decentralized Data Science, to which characteristics and functions typical of blockchain technology have been added: decentralized control, immutability, creation and transfer of assets.

The members of the Foundation have foreseen that as the database and the success of the project progress, the association will even proceed towards the dissolution of the association with complete decentralization also from an organizational point of view.

The application areas of the decentralized database concern the management of intellectual property in sectors such as fintech, banking, payment, energy, supply chain and government.

# Decentralized Distributed Database: Governance

To avoid the risk of utopia, the IPDB model has chosen to be a voluntary association (which is called the IPDB Foundation): guaranteeing legal personality to the network and in this way the association can legally stipulate contracts, but, so that there are no ulterior motives or personal profit purposes, it was decided that more than half of the custodians should be constituted by other non-profit organizations or public bodies. Likewise, to avoid the risk of being subject to the laws of a single country, less than half of the custodians can come from the same country. All custodians then have to be publicly committed to building a decentralized Internet.

## Blockchain and Reality: Be Careful About Expectations

The blockchain has been gathering increasing attention for some time, it can perhaps be said that despite being a complex technology it has become a mainstream theme, the issues of blockchain are also dealt with by large newspapers, radios and televisions that rarely bring focus on such innovative technologies. In many cases, the blockchain is proposed as the solution to problems and needs that come from afar and that have never really been satisfied by traditional technologies. The expectations, not only of companies but of consumers, of citizens, towards the possibilities of the blockchain have increased a lot. On the one hand, this situation favors debate and the growth of attention also by those who are working on the development of new solutions, but on the other hand it creates a dangerous situation because some of the beneficial effects that are today attributed to the blockchain they are the result of misunderstandings or a distorted reading of the very important possibilities of this technology. The risk is that if the blockchain is now brought into the palm of the hand for what it can do, if it does not keep these promises in an equally radical way it can be put aside. But it is important to highlight that some expectations and the solution of some needs are not to be attributed to the blockchain. Let's try and see some.

## Food certification

In the context of agri-food, blockchain is finding growing consensus, precisely because it can provide guarantees of reliability on often complex and often very fragmented supply chains, not only for the size of the companies but for the culture of the organizations or countries in which they operate. The blockchain is a platform that guarantees the certainty, the immutability, the transparency of the data that accompanies the production. But we must not think that the blockchain is intrinsically itself a guarantee of quality, which can by itself provide not only the certification but the quality of the product. The blockchain certifies the data and guarantees its identity and transparency for all actors. But if the original data does not correctly represent the product that goes into production, if that data are incorrect the blockchain does not correct it. On the contrary, the blockchain guarantees that incorrect data are kept intact throughout the supply chain. The transparency of the blockchain is a possible corrective, everyone can see that data, and everyone can (if they are in a position to do so) ascertain its value and propose a correction and a corrective (towards those who put it into production) but intrinsically it is not the blockchain that is able to ascertain the quality of the data. The blockchain guarantees the management process of that data for all participants.

## Smart contracts and notaries

Another area in which it is important to set the spaces and expectations linked to the blockchain well is that of smart contracts. Smart contracts that rely on the blockchain can bring enormous benefits to businesses, organizations and public administrations. The prospects are indisputable and sectors such as insurance, logistics and procurement are already achieving important benefits. Here too remains a point of utmost attention in the phase of transition from the real, physical and digital world, in the certainty of providing correct information by subjects, persons or companies, correct and correctly identified. On the management of this passage the scenario is still open, and the debate is still open. The function of the notary can play an important role in providing those guarantees that allow processes based on smart contracts to start with secure data or with data shared by all the parties involved or by all the players in a supply chain. Also in this case it is not the blockchain that can ascertain the truthfulness or quality of an information.

The blockchain guarantees its incorruptibility, protects the data from possible violations and transparently exposes it to all the actors involved and, in this way, speeds up the possible identification of errors but it is not an intelligent system to guarantee the quality of the data.

# Where Are We in the Development of the Blockchain on the Market?

The blockchain is a rather recent phenomenon that has experienced an important series of accelerations and that has created many expectations. At the same time, developing and implementing the blockchain is not an easy task and no single company can make it happen. For everyone, producers and companies or user organizations, blockchain is an ecosystem phenomenon of a collaborative type. Also for this reason, if on the one hand the level of attention that accompanies the blockchain is very high, on the other, the number of concrete cases of projects actually in production in companies and organizations is still quite low.

In this regard, it is interesting to see the interpretation of the evolution of the blockchain that Capgemini offers in the research "Does blockchain hold the key to a new age of supply chain transparency and trust?".

There are three waves of the blockchain according to Capgemini:

1. awareness: started in 2011 and it's still ongoing. Businesses and organizations are trying to understand, to develop knowledge;

2. experimentation: according to Capgemini it started in 2017 and lasted until 2020. Businesses and organizations are working at PoC to create skills, forms of collaboration, devise new consortia, with the goal of fully understanding the potential and criticalities of blockchain;

3. transformation: started in 2019 and it will accompany us until 2025. In this period the blockchain will transform the ways of relationship, integration and collaboration bringing innovation at multiple levels: technology, data management, governance.